VIETNAMESE WOMEN AT WAR

MODERN
WAR
STUDIES

Theodore A. Wilson

General Editor

Raymond A. Callahan

J. Garry Clifford

Jacob W. Kipp

Jay Luvaas

Allan R. Millett

Dennis Showalter

Series Editors

VIETNAMESE WOMEN AT WAR

FIGHTING FOR HO CHI MINH AND THE REVOLUTION

SANDRA C. TAYLOR

University Press of Kansas

Published by the University Press of Kansas (Lawrence, Kansas 66049), which was organized by the Kansas Board of Regents and is operated and funded by Emporia State University, Fort Hays State University, Kansas State University, Pittsburg State University, the University of Kansas, and Wichita State University

Library of Congress Cataloging-in-Publication Data

British Library Cataloguing in Publication Data is available.

The paper used in this publication meets the minimum requirements of the American National Standard for Permanence of Paper for Printed Library Materials Z39.48-1984.

Taylor, Sandra C.

Vietnamese women at war : fighting for Ho Chi Minh and the revolution / Sandra C. Taylor.

p. cm. — (Modern war studies)

Includes bibliographical references (p.   ) and index.

ISBN 0-7006-0927-X (alk. paper)

1. Vietnamese Conflict, 1961–1975—Women—Interviews. 2. Vietnamese Conflict, 1961–1975—Personal narratives, Vietnamese. 3. Women—Vietnam—Interviews. I. Title. II. Series.

DS559.8.W6T39   1999

959.704'3'082—dc21   98-35715

                                                            CIP

Printed in the United States of America

10 9 8 7 6 5 4 3 2 1

To my husband, Russell Wilhelmsen,
whose first trip to Vietnam was in 1992.
He has learned to love the land and
respect its people as much as I.

CONTENTS

• • • • • • • • • • • • • •

A photo gallery follows page 70.

ACKNOWLEDGMENTS

• • • • • • • • • • • •

My work owes much to those who have helped me. Douglas Pike, Geoffrey S. Smith, and Klancy deNevers read and commented on earlier versions of this work. Hoang Ngoc Nguyen of Ho Chi Minh City and Salt Lake City provided a keen eye in detecting numerous errors, and he added his own reminiscences. I would also like to thank James Reckner, director of the Center for the Study of the Vietnam Conflict, at Texas Tech in Lubbock, for his assistance. Kathryn Fuller, the archivist at Texas Tech in October 1996, who spent many hours with me finding materials, and her able assistant, now interim archivist, Jim Ginther, gave me great support, not only with the papers in the Pike Collection, but also with other materials—microfiche from the Cornell Archives—being accessed as I worked. Since the Pike Collection was in the process of being cataloged as I arrived, their help and insights were extremely useful.

Students Hung Tran and Thanh Quang Huynh of the University of Utah also gave me much needed assistance with Vietnamese, and Thanh helped me understand the Vietnamese culture today. His mother, Nguyen Thi Xuan Mai, provided invaluable assistance when I was in Vietnam. Other aid was offered by Matthew Briggs, Mike Hannigan, and Yu-Wen Huang, my undergraduate student research assistants. Yu-Wen Hwang was relentless in finding all those many errors in footnotes, punctuation, and sentence fragments. My companion through much of these travels, independent filmmaker Mel Halbach, has supported me in this project, helping me through many difficulties in traveling in Vietnam. He pursued his own project on the long-haired warriors as I worked on this manuscript, and we have benefited from each other's discoveries. My former student Eli Cawley, now a resident of Ho Chi Minh City, married to a Vietnamese woman, Nguyet, and father of a son, Claude, gave me many insights on contemporary customs and culture and the bits of history he has picked up in three years there. Other students, faculty, and "fellow Vietnam junkies" who accompanied me on two trips to Vietnam also deserve a debt of gratitude: Ray Gunn, B. Gale Dick, Peggy Battin, Brooke Hopkins, Anne Walthall, the late Elizabeth Mandersheid, David Green, and Pat Briggs. And, of course, I owe a great debt to Nguyen Thi Sau, without whom this project could not have come to fruition.

As always, I thank my husband, Russell Wilhelmsen, travel companion and technical assistant, whose patience with my computer illiteracy and tireless travel enthusiasm kept me going.

As I conclude this work, I must add the usual caveat that the opinions in this work are mine alone, as are the inevitable errors.

VIETNAMESE WOMEN AT WAR

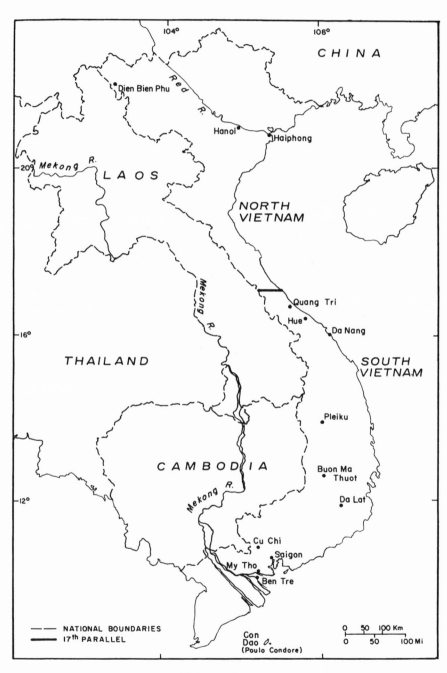

Vietnam at war

INTRODUCTION

• • • • • • • • • • • • • • • •

To look at her now, one would never believe her past. Dieu-Hong was a very attractive woman in her middle forties, her short black hair permed, her face attractively made up, lipstick on her lips. She wore Western-style fashions made for her in her favorite dress shop in Ho Chi Minh City, and she balanced her height of four feet, ten inches on three-inch heels. Her fingernails and toenails glistened with bright red nail polish. She was the quintessential urban sophisticate.

She was also very much a believer in Communism and in the doctrines of Ho Chi Minh. However much corruption pervaded the contemporary culture of her native land, it did not touch her home and had not altered her convictions. Her father had been a revolutionary, a supporter of Ho Chi Minh, and she followed in his footsteps. If a market economy was necessary now, that did not invalidate the premises for which the members of the resistance had fought.

It was as we discussed the events of April 1975 that I gained a glimpse of the fighter she had been. She had returned to Hanoi from higher education in the Soviet Union just in time for what became the final campaign to liberate South Vietnam, to unite the country and free it from foreign oppression, the one that became the "Ho Chi Minh campaign." She applied for permission to join the People's Army of Vietnam (PAVN) and camouflaged her sex through a clever twist on her name, omitting the telltale "Thi," which indicated that she was female. Her application was accepted, and the commander did not turn her away even when he recognized her real identity. She knew how to fire a rifle and had won medals for marksmanship during her university years. Her feet might not be tough enough to walk the many miles south, but she was highly patriotic and anxious to serve her country. When her feet gave out, the men in her unit carried her in a hammock, and they guarded her while she slept.

I did not know how difficult her military service had been until I visited the city of Hue with her, twenty years later. "Dieu-Hong, have you ever been here before?" I asked her. She replied that she had, during the Ho Chi Minh campaign, but for only two days, which she had spent in the hospital being treated for gunshot wounds.

She downplayed her own valor, however. She was not, she insisted, a "long-haired warrior," the appellation given to the women who had fought for their country during the war with the United States, providing not only logistical support, propaganda, and intelligence services, but firepower as well. She had, after all, been out of the country for almost the entire war. But she would take me to meet the real long-haired warriors, and together she and I would unravel the story of Vietnam's female fighters, who supported the Communist cause throughout the land.[1]

The history of the South Vietnamese women who, along with their northern sisters, fought for the National Liberation Front against the Saigon regime and the American government is mentioned in few books. Although men were the vast majority of the combatants in the country's many wars, there were women warriors in Vietnam during nearly a half-century of conflict, and the tradition dated from the beginning of the country's history. The women of the war with America are aging now, their stories fast disappearing as Vietnam modernizes and the war fades from memory. The women clad in black pajamas who raised the children, tilled the soil, and sold goods at markets throughout the land are still there, however, a legacy of the past in a land whose population is still more than 80 percent peasant. In my previous travels to Vietnam, I had not associated them with conflict, but now I sought to hear their stories, to understand how they had come to be called by Ho Chi Minh the "long-haired warriors," and to learn how they and the northern women had helped the Communist cause to victory.

* * *

My search began with a trip to the home of many of the first long-haired warriors, the village of Dinh Thuy, in Ben Tre Province, about sixty miles south of Ho Chi Minh City. As I was driven there, I noticed that the rice paddies and few open areas were dotted with the ubiquitous water buffalo, young boys astride. Small round ponds, former bomb craters, were now used for fish cultivation, perhaps the only useful by-product of the many years of war, defoliation, devastation, and death. The countryside was lush and green, densely populated with peasants working at the many tasks associated with wet rice agriculture. The elderly and small children sold goods beside the road.

The foliage was a postwar product; the Mekong Delta had been heavily bombed before 1975, since it was a center of resistance to French as well as American power. A majority of the peasantry had supported the nationalist/Communist cause, the forces of revolution. The Viet-Nam Doc Lap Dong Minh, or Viet Minh (League for the Independence of Vietnam), of the French war and the revolutionaries termed Viet Cong by President Ngo Dinh Diem during the American war were ideological ancestors. They shared a goal, to free their country and unify it under one Vietnamese government.[2] These people had, after 1960, become members of the National Front for the Liberation of Vietnam (NLF), which they called the Front. Some of the women I would meet were members of the Communist Party, but many others who fought were not; yet all had struggled for freedom. The women of Dinh Thuy had sacrificed to a degree that would have been unimaginable to an American, but they had endured for the cause of independence.[3] The unification of their country would also make possible the reuniting of families split since the Geneva Accords of 1954. They could not understand why Americans, foreigners, had made war on them.

In November 1995, Ben Tre, famous as the coconut province, looked as though physical memories of the war had been eradicated by time. Half the city had been destroyed in the Tet Offensive, and almost all the inhabitants had lost family members. The brilliant green rice paddies were deceptive. The area had been defoliated by Agent Orange and its cousins, Agents Blue and White: the chemicals remained in the soil, hence in the food chain, and a disproportionate number of pregnancies were affected by them.[4] Perhaps twenty more years would pass before this land, and much of the south, would be totally free from their deadly legacy. The women of the delta still had a high rate of stillbirths and bore many deformed infants.[5] But there were other problems that people faced: inadequate medical care, the lack of safe water supplies, not enough food for all, the absence of flood and drought relief, and a very low standard of living.

It had been ten years since my first visit to this area, fifteen years after the defoliation program ended. The replanted trees had not yet reached their prewar heights. Many small children gave proof of the ability of the human race to replenish itself, and indeed overpopulation, not the extinguishing of life, was a problem now. Despite the efforts of the branches of the Vietnam Women's Union throughout the land, the birth rate was still higher than the government wanted, especially in rural areas like this. Peasants have always relied on large families to till the fields and care for the elderly, and they still do. Also, women are still pressured to have a son, to ensure the continuation of the family line. Like the trees, the population grew back.

I went to Dinh Thuy in 1995 to gather information from women who had participated in the uprisings begun in January 1960 by Nguyen Thi Dinh, who became the highest ranking female member of the National Liberation Front's armed forces, the People's Liberation Armed Forces (PLAF). She commanded and inspired women throughout the South to join the fight against the "Saigon puppet troops," as the Communist Vietnamese referred to the armed forces of Ngo Dinh Diem's regime. She was awarded the appellation "long-haired warrior" after the successful uprisings, the *dong khoi*, in Ben Tre Province in January 1960. The sobriquet was later applied to all the women of the southern resistance by Ho Chi Minh himself.[6] The women of Dinh Thuy had been important participants in the uprisings, and hence the village was a good place for me to begin my search.

Arriving at Dinh Thuy presaged many later meetings arranged by the Women's Union. The head of the village association welcomed us with a speech full of statistics and goals, and I responded with remarks about my gratitude for their willingness to meet with me. But in this case, the preliminaries were speeded up: many elderly women were already seated around a low table waiting to speak, so our translator interrupted and we began the interviews. Even the youngest of the women was in her fifties in 1995, and many were in their late seventies or eighties. Their hair was gray; their faces were wrinkled; their bodies were thin and stooped. They were uniformly attired in black trousers, but some wore silken blouses with mandarin collars and long sleeves instead of the usual simple cotton shirt; a few had the traditional checkered neck scarf of the region around their necks. One woman had teeth stained black with betel juice, a combination of nut and lime that dulls the pain of rotting teeth and infirm bodies. Since their gray hair was now gathered at the nape of their necks in a knot, they scarcely resembled the women they were thirty years earlier, who with loose long black hair had tormented the forces of the Army of the Republic of Vietnam (ARVN) and its American advisers, staunch opponents of Communism.

We were accompanied by Nguyen Thi Sau, our "minder," interpreter, helper, facilitator, and friend. (Nguyen Thi Sau is the pseudonym this woman selected to preserve her anonymity.) She not only translated and spelled names, but also helped me understand the dynamics of many situations, who was "very important" and why—Party member, war heroine, very elderly woman, someone with family high in the echelons of politics in Ho Chi Minh City or Hanoi. The Vietnamese government did not oppose such travel as this trip to Dinh Thuy, but at that time it still preferred to know where foreigners were. Setting up the meetings also required considerable effort.

The women in this village and elsewhere described the horrors of war and paused only when they talked of the separation from children, the deaths of loved ones, personal torture, or the terrors of American bombing. Perhaps they had told these stories to foreigners before, but sometimes the Vietnamese prefer to bury memories, since to tell them recalls the pain they suffered, and they prefer to look toward the future. Although Nguyen Thi Sau had cautioned me not to cry when hearing the women's stories, sometimes both she and I had tears in our eyes. Some of the women also wept at stories that were particularly horrifying, especially if the narrator was in obvious physical pain.

As the hours passed at Dinh Thuy, we became more uncomfortable. The backless wooden bench on which we sat strained our spines, and our knees were cramped under the low table. We knew that we could never have squatted on our heels to rest, as the curious onlookers did. By the time the formal interviewing had ended, some twenty younger women had joined us, as had many children. The arrival of these foreigners, "good Americans" who had not fought in the war, and this sophisticated and politically important city woman from the former Saigon was certainly a big event in the village.

The women of Dinh Thuy had been members of the original group of long-haired warriors: they had struggled with great ingenuity against the Saigon and American troops; and they, but not their children, husbands, or parents, had survived the high-tech war the Americans had fought. The countless bombings, defoliations, imprisonments, and tortures had intimidated them but not broken their spirits. Their ways of resistance were ingenious: they were the unseen enemy who planted *punji* stakes in the trails, hid fighters in underground pits in their huts, and served as liaisons with the guerrillas in the jungle. To see them now, some thirty-five years after the great uprisings in Ben Tre, brought home to us the unevenness of the victory. By late 1995, the benefits of *doi moi* were apparent in Ho Chi Minh City, Hanoi, and smaller cities. For these elderly peasants, however, life was peaceful but little else had changed, although motorbikes were replacing bicycles and foot traffic, even in the villages, and electricity was being extended to the countryside. The proximity of this village to Ben Tre, My Tho, and Ho Chi Minh City provided access to the emerging market economy, and people were devising ingenious ways of making money.[7] What would their beloved Uncle Ho have said?

The four hours at Dinh Thuy passed quickly. All too soon we were rushed off to a bounteous lunch that the villagers had prepared, featuring all the local delicacies—specialties they would never have eaten unless they were entertaining very important guests. Only a very few of the dishes, including cassavas and bananas roasted over a fire, were true peasant fare, certainly not such extravagances as shrimp, pork, and even rice, which was reserved for the guerrillas during the war. Cassavas had sustained the women and children left behind. But we had no time to enjoy the food, for rain threatened. Our driver told Nguyen Thi Sau that we had to leave; a wet and muddy road would be impassable, and we risked missing the ferry back to Ben Tre. Since some of the elderly women had walked considerable distances from surrounding hamlets to talk to me, we also had to be considerate of their need to return before the monsoon rains began. As we departed, they tried to press bunches of bananas and other fruits on us; it was embarrassing to be offered so much when they had so little. They received assistance from their families and the Women's Union, but this was not a rich district and no one lived in abundance.[8] Their margin of survival was very meager, and there was little we could do to help. The gift one woman gave me, a spoon and fork carved from a coconut husk, was touching and saddening.[9]

To Westerners, these women appear to be victims, lonely, aged before their time, living in poverty. They have not achieved political power, and their place in the family is much the same as before. Today's government has emphasized their victimization in the war, but this emphasis on "woman-as-victim" is not a real indication of women achieving power.[10] The death of Nguyen Thi Dinh brought her significant recognition throughout Vietnam, beyond the confines of the Women's Union. The museum in Ben Tre and the women's museums in Ho Chi Minh City and Hanoi devote space to the uprising and her leadership role. She was little known to Americans during the war—if, indeed, they had heard of her at all. The other long-haired warriors were even more invisible, the "peasants by day, soldiers by night" feared by Americans and ARVN soldiers alike. The women of the wartime generation are dying, and their stories with them.

This work is in no sense a comprehensive account of all that Vietnam's Communist women did in the long wars against the French and the Americans. My interviews did not cover the entire country, and they were done in the presence of a Communist interpreter. The women did not give me their true feelings, but rather a dramatized account of their heroism, twenty or thirty years earlier. Since I was unable to interview people at random on the streets, I did not get a valid sample. Nor did I interview many overseas Vietnamese, whose stories are different. This work is a preliminary attempt to understand the women warriors, to set them in their culture, and to appreciate them as powerful participants in a major twentieth-century war.

1

. . . .

REVOLUTIONARY WOMEN

"When war comes, even women have to fight." This ancient saying of the Vietnamese was demonstrated in the extreme during the war fought between North Vietnam and its Communist allies in South Vietnam and the United States and its allies in the Republic of Vietnam in the south, a conflict that lasted from 1945 to 1975.[1] A woman who exemplified this slogan and personified the role that revolutionary women should play was Ut Tich, a resistance fighter against the French who then continued her ardor by participating in the conflict against the Americans. She carried out the three responsibilities, orders to women in the revolution to assume their share of the burden of warfare. She took responsibility for her household and raised her children, she carried on production so the soldiers could be fed, and she fought in place of her husband when he went off to war. These dicta were practiced more commonly in the North than in the South because everyone was mobilized there for the war against the Americans. But they were the guidelines that the Communist Party promoted, and Ut Tich, a southern woman, obeyed them.[2]

The three responsibilities grew out of the words of Ho Chi Minh, who exhorted his followers: "Nothing is more precious than independence and freedom," a slogan still visible on billboards in Vietnam in 1991. If his interpretation of freedom differed from that of the West, it did not matter: independence was something about which no one differed.

Ut Tich's story, an account of the life of a heroine well known to school-children in both North and South Vietnam during the war, serves as an example and an introduction to the lives of the long-haired warriors. In 1930, a female child named Nguyen Thi Ut was born to an impoverished family in Tam Ngai, Cau Ke District, Tra Vinh Province, a very remote and im-poverished area. Her parents were tenant farmers who suffered from mal-nutrition and overwork. Her father, according to the story, died of exhaustion as he labored for his French masters. As a small child, Ut was hired out to a wealthy landowner, for whom she labored all day for bare sustenance. Poorly fed, she often was tied up and beaten for her low productivity. When the August Revolution broke out in 1945 and the country was in turmoil, she took the opportunity to flee to her uncle, only to discover that he was another tyrannical oppressor. But when she found what she thought might be valuable documents, she gave them to a local cadre whom she knew. This person, a Communist official, told her of the plans that Ho Chi Minh (then Nguyen Ai Quoc) had devised for achieving victory over the French and their allies. Ut soon ran away from her uncle and, at fifteen, became a liaison for the resistance fighters in the district. The next year, she informed her com-rades of an impending attack by the French; as a reward, she was allowed to participate in an ambush. The guerrillas killed seven French soldiers and captured numerous weapons and ammunition. Ut fought in frequent en-gagements and did proselytizing and liaison work.[3]

When Ut Tich married,[4] her husband, an ethnic Khmer, joined a local armed force serving the French. Ut Tich became a scout and a liaison worker for the Communist Party— both she and her husband were secretly Com-munists. After the defeat of the French in 1954, Ut Tich and her husband recognized a new enemy, the Americans and the "Saigon puppet troops." She organized face-to-face struggles in which women confronted soldiers and police as a group and demanded compensation for their dead, the reduction of taxes, and an end to the draft. She worked to "reeducate" sol-diers of the Saigon government to join the resistance. In addition, she took a more active role in the war, becoming an ambulance attendant, and both she and her husband were guerrillas. The total enemy she herself killed—

like the later body counts of the American forces—began to mount. The numbers themselves took on a mythic quality.

By this time, Ut Tich had six children, the youngest still an infant. One day as she was going to market, she saw an enemy company passing by; she took her children home to hide them and informed her guerrilla group of the hostile forces. The guerrillas plotted an ambush, in which Ut Tich killed two enemy soldiers and, according to the story, wounded many others.

In a later exploit, her wily maneuvers enabled her to seize an enemy outpost. She became acquainted with the commander, promised to cook him an elaborate banquet, plied the soldiers with liquor, and then seized the commander's rifle and took him and his men prisoners, disarming them and adding the weapons to the cache of the guerrillas.

On the eve of the lunar new year, Tet 1965, Ut Tich, although pregnant, led an armed propaganda group to a nearby town. She ordered her men to withdraw and, with a tommy gun slung across her back, then distributed leaflets of the National Liberation Front. The village was under the Saigon government's control, and many of its young men fought for its army. When the villagers asked her name, she told them to call her "Cousin Liberation." Another account of her exploits relates that she "fought the enemy in all circumstances and by every means, sowing permanent panic among the[m]." A true long-haired warrior, Nguyen Thi Ut Tich earned the title Heroine of the Liberation Army in early 1965.[5] A booklet entitled "Brilliant Examples to Emulate: The Distinguished Services of Women-Fighters" narrated her story and those of other outstanding women guerrillas, and in lists of heroines of the war in the South, her name is always prominently featured. The purpose of writing stories such as Ut Tich's was to inspire other women to follow the example of these fearless killers and to dramatize their cause to their supporters around the world.[6] A true martyr to the cause, Ut Tich died during the war, probably in 1965. She had fulfilled all the goals of the "three responsibilities": she bore six children, she kept the household going so production would be maintained and the resistance forces supplied, and she carried and used a weapon.

Accounts of the lives of women like Ut Tich and her comrades verge on the incredulous to a Western observer unused to wars of resistance or the extraordinary abilities that such conflict demands. No doubt, many stories have been embellished with time, while others have an almost mythic quality that reflects the passage of thirty years or more. Tiny women carried loads weighing 200 pounds across rivers, up and down mountains, and through dense jungles. They suffered tortures beyond belief, cruelties administered in horrifying ways: they were beaten with sharp green bamboo rods, their sexual organs were mutilated with electric shocks, pointed sticks were inserted under their fingernails. Yet they insisted after the war that they had never revealed a word, never betrayed their comrades. They learned military tactics, some in the North joining the People's Army of Vietnam and those in the South fighting with local militias, the People's Liberation Armed Forces, and the guerrillas of the National Liberation Front. Yet they were also loving mothers and loyal wives who did not forget their Confucian heritage.

These Vietnamese women were part of the Communists' "people's war," a conflict that involved all members of society. Virtually every interrogation of prisoners of war or those who defected to the South under its *chieu hoi* program asked about the Women's Liberation Association of the village to which the prisoner or defector belonged. Who was its head? Who were the members? If the prisoner was a woman, she was asked many times why she had joined the National Liberation Front, what her tasks were, and who her comrades were. Although peasant women cultivated and harvested paddy rice and raised farm animals, these women were not the traditional passive, religious wives—timid in public, lacking in social consciousness, and, even if oppressed, more used to enduring than fighting back.[7] They followed the "three obediences" of Confucius, obeying first the father, then the husband, then the oldest son. They observed filial piety, honoring their ancestors, their parents when they were children, their husband's ancestors after they married. How could such women go to war?

In interviewing Vietnamese women who had participated in the country's resistance, I found that they drew on their land's 2,000-year history as well as the very recent past. They sometimes cited the Trung sisters, victorious over China in C.E. 40, but martyrs to the cause of Vietnam.

In order to learn about the revolutionary women of the French and American wars, I had to ask the women themselves, peasants and city women, illiterate and intellectual. This involved drawing on their memories of events twenty-five years or more in the past. The broad outlines of modern Vietnamese history are the context for these women warriors: many became fighters for liberation because it was a family tradition. France as a colonial power had been hated by a majority of Vietnamese ever since their land had been colonized in 1868. During World War II, Japanese occupation in 1940 and 1941 brought a new group of colonial oppressors, whom some women remembered for their cruelty. The end of that conflict did not bring peace, and after the French war (First Indochina War) ended in 1954, many people joined in the struggle against the United States and its "lackey," the government of Ngo Dinh Diem. To them, the Americans were successors to the French, foreigners who wanted to impose their will on the Vietnamese people, the Saigon government and forces being mere puppets.

The Communist Party gave the resistance an ideology, an interpretation of history that justified people's suffering and enabled them to see victory as inevitable, however long that might take. As Vietnamese, they honored Ho Chi Minh as their savior more than they revered Karl Marx or Vladimir I. Lenin.[8] Ho was indeed a Communist and a longtime member of the Comintern, but he was also an ardent nationalist who became the father of his country, a legendary symbol of the selfless leader, and an ideological ruler who brought to his homeland a belief system that promised not only independence and unification, but also equality of men and women.[9]

Some women became revolutionaries during World War II, and some, who were exposed to socialist ideas while abroad, supported Communism even earlier. Since 1930, Party doctrine had encouraged women to believe that there was a place in the Party hierarchy for them, that they could be part of the government, and that they would not be tied to the home and the demands of husband and oppressive mother-in-law. But for most women, the promises made at the meeting of the Central Committee of the Eighth Plenum of the Indochinese Communist Party (ICP) on August 16, 1945, the day that Japan surrendered, were the most important. The Party proclaimed its advocacy of "universal suffrage, democratic liberties, equality among all ethnic groups and between men and women."[10] Ho Chi Minh urged all Vietnamese to work together—without discriminating on the basis of age, sex, or religion—in support of an insurrection for the winning of independence. When Ho Chi Minh established the mass organizations, he intended that they involve every member of society in groups that would promote revolution, inculcate national pride, combat the natural passivity of the peasantry, and overcome the dread of fighting a technologically superior enemy. The Communists, he believed, could surpass the Americans and South Vietnamese by their iron will, and the outcome of the conflict would seem to bear that out. Ho had spoken informally of an end to arranged marriages and of the opportunity for women to learn to read, study, participate in politics, and be truly men's equals. Northern Communist women still remembered his words in 1994.[11]

In the election held on January 6, 1946, the people supported Ho Chi Minh overwhelmingly. The election was to establish a government for Ho's newly established Democratic Republic of Vietnam, the successor to the French colonies of Tonkin, Annam, and Cochin China. That women were the equals of men had been demonstrated in the war against Japan, during which tribal women from the mountainous border with Laos had served as porters carrying supplies to the battlefront. The idea of equality, participation in the electorate, and an independence movement on terms of shared sacrifice drew in many women—especially urban, educated women. Yet Ho was even more popular in the countryside. For peasants, the Party's promise of equality might mean an end to the ceaseless drudgery of agricultural work, stoop labor that aged them before their time. Peasant women organized in cells, engaged in self-criticism sessions at which they examined their own worth as believers and activists in the Communist Party, and criticized one another for failures of sufficient zeal and determination. The promise of universal suffrage and equality among all ethnic groups and between men and women heralded, at least in theory, a new order.[12] Despite the immense differences between the classical Confucian image of women and the ideology of Ho's revolution, urban women were essential and often willing recruits; they would be indispensable in wartime, since they lived among the enemy.

Ho's image of sacrifice and his saintly visage drew peasant women to him. This charismatic leader provided them with the determination to survive torture and imprisonment in the belief that victory would soon be theirs. He was the god of their civil religion, the image to whom they burned incense, a man worthy of residing on the shrine to their ancestors. Although very few women from the South actually saw him, and many were unable to read his writings, Ho's charisma stimulated them. His austere life of sacrifice was an inspiration, a model for their own. The idea of equality between men and women, which had been a slogan of the Indochinese Communist Party since its founding in 1930, held out hope even if the reality of the women's lives belied it.[13]

Questions about history, memory, and ideology inevitably appear in such a study as this. History was made and preserved by female peasants and prisoners who were part of the resistance and had no means of recording daily events in writing. Poems, the traditional form of literature in Vietnam, enabled them to remember and idealize the past. Chronology and individuals

were less important than the large picture of suffering, courage, determination, and ultimate victory. The honoring of one individual above others was
discouraged in Communist ideology, and few women were known outside
their own districts. However, if the emphasis on heroines in poems, songs,
and hagiographic tales portrayed the revolutionaries as a group or typified
them as doing "what any woman would do," specific individuals of the most
downtrodden class, like Ut Tich, might be heralded as models to be copied. Indeed, emulation became a goal, a motto, and captured documents
frequently referred to its desirability. A poem of heroism and sacrifice was
easily remembered and could be chanted despite prison guards' orders to
remain silent. It boosted morale and helped maintain courage, just as it must
have enraged prison guards and soldiers of the Saigon army. Poetry was a
living testimony to the willpower of the insurgents.[14]

One example shows the power of verse. Luong Thi Trang, a Ben Tre
woman arrested as a Communist agent by the regime of Ngo Dinh Diem in
1959 and held until 1973, admitted in an interview that she could not
remember the details of events that had occurred so long ago. A member of
the Women's Liberation Association, she had been moved from one prison
to another, her ten-year sentence doubled when she participated in a prison
demonstration, probably at the women's facility in Thu Duc District in the
outskirts of Saigon.[15] She had hoped to be released, but the officials just
moved her to another prison in an apparent attempt to break her will. This
system of frequent transfers was designed to break prisoners' morale and to
keep them from confiding in one another or planning an outbreak or rebellion. Women seem to have been able to endure imprisonment as well as or
better than men; their courage impressed their male comrades and, occasionally, their guards. Like other prisoners, Trang was tortured and abused,
and she suffered from malnutrition and disease, especially when she was
transferred to Con Dao, the prison on the island of Con Son.[16]

The male prisoners were so impressed with the bravery of the women in
Con Dao that they composed a poem for them. Trang still knew it by heart:

> Only the fire can know the age of the gold.
> We men respect the bravery of the Vietnamese women.
> Although you were put in jail, you did not withdraw.
> Although you lived under the rain of beatings,
> you did not betray the country. You look like the
> white flower blossoms in the dirty lake.

> Just to show your bravery and strength,
> your spirit is strong like steel.
> Although you are very soft and gentle
> and honest and sincere,
> the rain of blows cannot break your spirit.
> You have overcome many difficulties to come to victory.
> Only the fire can tell exactly the quality of gold.[17]

Poetry as a mechanism for remembering shaped the women's recollections of the past.[18] Some poems were inspirational, others referred to specific events, but they all served a useful function. They taught people Communist goals and expectations, but they were also wonderful ways to honor heroes and heroines, to pay tribute to their suffering. They could evoke a mood—tragic, ironic, humorous, or full of hatred—and recall the time and place of a specific past event. Poems could transcend the immediate and make heroes of those anonymous people who suffered and died for their beliefs—or were random victims of an increasingly violent war. Hence memory of an event was conveyed in a specific form that might be shaped to serve political ends. Vietnamese culture had a strong oral tradition, since for most of the country's history the population was largely illiterate. Suffering, especially that of women, was memorialized to transform the enemy into monsters, foreign imperialists, or "puppets." Women, in such a tradition, were not victims but heroines.

The political program of the National Liberation Front of the South, written about 1966, called for free general elections with universal, equal, direct suffrage and secret ballots. It also demanded the enforcement of equality between men and women in every aspect of life: equal pay for equal work, protection of pregnant women, and a two-month maternity leave with full pay before and after childbirth. It also called for a policy of actively favoring and training women cadres.[19] The first constitution of the North, the Democratic Republic of Vietnam, made law of many of these concepts, which had been goals of radical women for decades.[20] Women might exercise some control over their own lives, have a say in their choice of spouse, perhaps even in the number of children they bore—or even choose not to marry. It promised, during wartime, freedom to move about as soldiers, propagandists, intelligence operatives, and liaisons. For many, like Trang, joining the Party was the logical course to take, following in the footsteps of family and history. Trang paid a high price, her long imprisonment ruling out any hope of marriage and a family.

The question of special rights for women, such as protection and time off for pregnancy, maternity leave with two months off before and after giving birth, was an alluring promise that held perils as well. If women needed unique privileges because of their sex, that made them in a sense less equal than men. Their need for protected status might preclude their becoming high ranking Party officials. Equal pay for equal work was one thing, but the promise of an end to polygamy, arranged marriages, and child marriage was also desirable. The tasks they could undertake during wartime provided them with independent lives: moving about freely as liaisons, working as propagandists, and proselytizing for the Party. The one thing that could be promised but not delivered on was true equality, the opportunity to take positions at the top of the political order. This would have to wait until men gave up their traditional assumptions about women's roles.

Yet to take at face value a story such as Trang's, recounted to a sympathetic recorder more than twenty years after the events, raises many questions. First, how can the interviewer, as an American, understand the Vietnamese cultural context and the "truth" of what this woman or other women said? Did the woman herself remember the events of her long period of imprisonment? At certain points, she admitted that she did not, that the lengthy incarceration had caused memories of her life to run together in her mind. She may even have confused what happened to her with stories she heard from other women. There was no way to cross-check her history with other accounts, and when I questioned others, their stories were much the same.[21] It was impossible to talk with her again, and I could not interview her without a Party guide. The women shared an ideological bond: they had been the victims of the Americans and the South Vietnamese; they were members of the Women's Union and the Communist Party. Their stories had to jibe with the official version of events. Hence questions relating to the tension between history and memory are germane to this study.[22]

Some cognitive psychologists have concluded that memories are not replays of actual facts from the past, but "reconstructions" that serve present needs.[23] In other words, people remember what is useful to their lives today—magnifying some things, forgetting others, shaping the whole to give purpose to the past. When one narrates one's life story, events of the distant past take on a quality differing from the reality of the experience. Oral histories of revolutionary women in Vietnam are shaped by the familiarity of the interviewer with the interviewees, understanding of culture and shared history, intonations of meaning hidden within language, even subtle nuances in the shared experience of villagers in one locale that differed from that of peasants some distance away. Contemporary events having to do with the victory of Communism and its one-party rule also demand stories of heroism and dedication to the death that promote the survival and continued triumph of a belief system that has been unable to deliver as much as it promised. Hence these women's memories, stories of events twenty to thirty years earlier, are not falsifications, but paeans to the glories of a particular ideology, testaments to the righteousness of their cause, testimonies to the need to persist against what these women saw as the cruelties of a foreign imperialist and its local supporters, even a justification for life as it is lived today.

Other analyses of history and memory stress different elements. The historian David Thelen has stated that "in each construction of a memory, people reshape, omit, distort, combine, and reorganize details from the past in an active and subjective way. They mix pieces from the present with elements from different periods in the past." People even subconsciously update memories as their comprehension of the past changes. Thelen also explained that the brain has no central storage facility to hold bins of information. Hence memory is triggered by associations, present needs, and circumstances.[24] In this very cursory examination of a complicated subject lies the reality of the oral histories that form a large part of the research for this work. The stories might not be literally true, but they represent what people want to remember and what serves their present needs.

One may ask why Vietnamese women had to describe themselves and their comrades as especially heroic and why, after the war they fought has faded from public consciousness, they sought to enshrine it. The answer lies in their sense of themselves, in Vietnamese gender roles, and in women's position in the history of their country. Few books in English have mentioned the Women's Liberation Association, the Vietnam Women's Union, the role of women in the National Liberation Front, or their participation in the war. Until the publication of her memoirs, Nguyen Thi Dinh was virtually unknown outside Vietnam, and Madame Nguyen Thi Binh, the representative of the NLF at the Paris peace negotiations in 1973, gained world attention as a spokesperson for the NLF cause and an advocate of peace as she traveled throughout the Third World; she was the only Vietnamese woman visible in the West, and she was not a warrior. That a woman, Nguyen

Thi Dinh, actually commanded troops and was the deputy commander of the forces of the National Liberation Front remained unknown in the West until after the war had ended. Lesser known but equally important women were not known at all in the West.

By 1994, the major women's history museums stressed the need to preserve the history not only of such heroines as Nguyen Thi Dinh and Madame Binh, but also of the common women of the Front, such as Ut Tich. They wanted children to know the country's past and the role that women played in achieving liberation. Although it was a "people's war," it was, as all wars are, dominated by men, who are well served by official histories and memorialized in major historical monuments and the national museums. It is women who must create and tend their own historical record. Museums, histories, and word of mouth are attempts to achieve this.[25]

Aside from memory and ideology, another factor enters into Vietnamese women's sense of themselves. Vietnamese myth and tradition stress the role of several strong women who helped save the country. The women's museums in Hanoi and Ho Chi Minh City open with a dramatic presentation on the Trung sisters, Trung Trac and Trung Nhi. When Trung Trac's husband, Thi Sach, a scholar, was killed by a Chinese governor, To Dinh, the Trung sisters moved to take revenge. In c.e. 40, Trung Trac was proclaimed queen after the army that she and her sister had led defeated the Chinese forces. During the rebellion, some twelve other women generals also led troops and fought against the invader. When, two years later, the Chinese returned to the Red River Delta, the Trungs committed suicide by drowning themselves in the Hai River.[26] A temple in Hanoi, the Hai Ba Trung, honors their memory.[27] Despite the sisters' ultimate defeat, Vietnamese today know their story and revere them as heroines who displayed traditional Vietnamese values of courage and resistance—despite a tradition of female subservience. In 248, Lady Trieu An, also known as Trieu Thi Trinh, a giantess with breasts allegedly three feet long, led another struggle against China. She supposedly threw her breasts over her shoulders and tied them down as she led the men into battle. Her downfall came when the enemy learned that she hated filth and crudeness. The opposing Chinese general sent his men into action filthy and naked, and then put symbols of penises over their huts. Lady Trieu An ran away, disgusted.[28]

Vietnam also has an origin myth of a powerful sea god, Lac Long Quan, and a beautiful goddess, Au Co. Their offspring, a hundred children, were divided between the two parents, one-half going to the sea with their father, the other half to the mountains with their mother. The Vietnamese people describe themselves as the offspring of the sea dragon and the fairy. For our purposes, it is sufficient to note that the offspring of the goddess Au Co became the legendary Hung kings.[29]

The Chinese introduced the teachings of Confucius as they conquered their southern neighbor. The Vietnamese learned that women were impossible to educate, should be confined within the family compound, and were men's inferior. Sayings such as "a hundred daughters are not worth one son" emphasized the reality of life for women, whether they were nobles or peasants. Women were bound by the Confucian precept to have a pure spirit and be a virgin before marriage and live chastely afterward, even if the husband died. They were to live by the "three obediences": at home, obey the father; leaving home, obey the husband; when the husband dies, obey the son. Women were to follow the "four virtues": work hard, care for their physical appearance, use appropriate speech, and master proper behavior.[30] Hundreds of precepts governed their lives.[31]

Such admonitions would seem to rule out a role for most women in combat. Most were illiterate, and their large families and poor health would not have allowed them to stray far from home even if they wished to. They had to tend the family altar and cater to the wishes of their mothers-in-law, and their only duty aside from home and field was to go to market. Although marketing was a task of the lowest status in a Confucian society, it was a necessity for daily life. In the market, women could gossip as well as barter or sell their goods, gather information to pass along to insurgents, and even demonstrate against corrupt officials. This opportunity would prove useful to the liberation movement. Although women traveled considerable distances in their trading activities, their work still did not elevate them to the status of men. However, controlling the family pocketbook also gave them power.

Yet in some ways, Vietnamese women were more liberated than Indian or Chinese women. Commoners were not immolated on their husband's death, and they did not have bound feet. But in cultural traditions, much else was similar. Women had little chance to learn to read, yet there were some very well known poets, including Ba Huynh, Thanh Quan, Ho Xuan Huong, and Duong Thi Diem.[32] Although polygamy was not widespread, women had to accept their husband's concubines, if they were unable to bear a son, and husbands could take a second wife. Divorce was unthinkable for a woman, although a man could divorce his wife. Indeed, according to one scholar, Vietnamese men were "second to none" in imposing a double standard on women. They did what they wished and brought their own concubines home; their wives could say nothing and had to remain faithful.[33] Women's lives were filled with unremitting toil, for women worked in the rice paddies along with their children and husbands and had to care for home and children.

Women's status changed under the different dynasties that ruled Vietnam, but since the time of the Trung sisters they were formally and informally subordinate to men. During the Ly Dynasty in the eleventh century, there were forced marriages and polygamy was made legal, although few practiced it. The custom of immolation of the king's wives upon his death was instituted. Subsequent dynasties continued this harsh rule and occasionally even increased the burden on women.[34]

The French entered Indochina first as missionaries, and then as conquerors. In the mid-nineteenth century, they divided the land of the Viets into three administrative divisions. Tonkin, in the north, held the city they made their capital, Hanoi. Annam, the central district, contained the historic capital of Hue, home of the Nguyen Dynasty. Cochin China, in the south, included Saigon, the "Paris of the East," a thriving metropolis that had once been a small fishing village. These three Vietnamese components, together with Laos and Cambodia, made up French Indochina, an important part of France's empire. The rulers followed a pattern of recruiting members of the local elite to become lower-level administrators and educating them in the Catholic faith and the French language. But their primary purpose was to exploit the resources of Indochina, especially those of the southern part of Vietnam, and that entailed utilizing its people, the majority of whom became laborers for their new rulers. The French colonial overlords did not consider the Vietnamese people to be their equals, which to them justified cruel treatment whenever necessary to compel obedience.

French conquest lowered women's status below what it had been under the Vietnamese dynasties. Women were "slaves of slaves," subordinate to their husbands, who were, in turn, chattels of the French.[35] Women were sometimes taken by the French as concubines and abandoned when their beauty faded. As inferiors, they could be used sexually as their masters wished, although the Catholic religion and French mores restrained more grotesque abuses. Women worked as hard as men on the French rubber plantations and were mistreated when they did not work hard enough. If they went to the infirmary, they might be forced to sleep with the French medical personnel.[36] The colonial government mandated the "preservation of old traditions, respect for Vietnam's ancestral customs and usages";[37] hence it endorsed and perpetuated women's submission as the previous Vietnamese dynasty had ordained it. When men opposed French rule, women joined with them in the resistance for many reasons, their mistreatment being just one of them. A few upper-class women went to France to study, and some learned of the French revolutionary tradition and of socialism as they pursued the classical education available at the Sorbonne.

Those at home became the subjects of a great discussion among Vietnamese intellectuals, who in the 1920s began to argue over the "question of women." Women had been suppressed for so long that most were illiterate and restricted to home and market; the intelligentsia held serious debates on the role of women in a modern society and wondered whether women were even capable of being educated. Although many men who would become revolutionaries were radical in their political consciousness, the great changes proposed in the status of women, essentially involving education and liberation from traditional gender roles, were too disturbing for most to accept. However, women-as-victim became a mode in which political discourse, forbidden by the French, could take place.[38] Many men were uncertain about to how to deal with the "women question," but it was a safe subject to debate because it treated the question of change in a politically neutral setting.

Some traditions were easier to abandon than others. By 1922, the writer Tran Quan Chi was composing articles for reform in newspapers such as *Southern Wind;* he called for an end to arranged and early marriages and polygamy. But neither he nor anyone else questioned premarital chastity, the axiom of fidelity throughout marriage and into widowhood, or the concepts of obedience and submissiveness.[39]

The introduction of Communism into the land inhabited by the Vietnamese people through the writings of Ho Chi Minh and his vanguard of revolutionaries had some appeal to women. But although it could potentially win female converts, the ideology presented many problems. Feudalism was cruel and degrading, and most considered independence from France necessary, but Communism posed special challenges for women, whose traditional roles had always been those of wife and mother. As the story of Luong Thi Trang indicates, taking part in the resistance could present circumstances under which women might have to postpone or even abandon the hope of marriage and children. In a society deeply wedded to family and children, this was a cruel fate. Ho did not demand it, but being part of the resistance might necessitate it.

The tenets of Communism and the teachings of Ho Chi Minh brought advantages and problems. Many women feared being regarded as "loose" if they consorted freely with men, as they would in fighting a guerrilla war. But there were promises: Ho Chi Minh called for an end to polygamy[40] and advocated the right of women to vote and participate in civic affairs: "Women are half the people. If women are not free, then the people are not free."[41] These ideas were inspiring and could be accepted by many. Ho's transformation into "Bac," father's older brother, made him an honorary member of one's family (and a safe figure in that he was, as far as anyone knew, unmarried and chaste),[42] thus elevating him to one worthy of allegiance. His promise of independence from France and America was the most inspiring pledge of all.

Nguyen Ai Quoc—the name by which Ho Chi Minh was known before 1941—had a primary task in the 1920s, the creation of a Communist Party in Vietnam. Assisted by the Comintern and operating from bases in southern China, he concealed the movement from the French secret police. His followers formed a youth group, Thanh Nien, that would in 1930 evolve into the Indochinese Communist Party. The Party included women from the outset, first informally, and then formally. "Mass organizations"—associations for workers, peasants, women, students, youth, artists and writers, even Buddhist monks—became part of the Party structure and were continued throughout the wars. Although Nguyen Ai Quoc opposed the idea of peasant uprisings because of the overwhelming power of the French, rebellions broke out in 1930 in Nghe An and Nghe Tinh, as starvation and mass discontent with colonial rule forced Quoc's hand. Joseph Stalin, his Soviet master, blamed him for their failure, although he had no role in their outbreak. In later years, Communist historians would call these uprisings the "Great Rehearsal" for the August Revolution of 1945, but at the time the toll on human life was enormous. The French had Nguyen Ai Quoc arrested in Shanghai, and although released by the British within the year, he was unable to take an active role in subsequent events. During the next few years, called in Vietnam the "white terror," the French rounded up all known revolutionaries and either killed or imprisoned them. Despite the fierce repression, the ICP, the first officially designated Marxist-Leninist organization in French Indochina, gained a foothold that it would not lose.

During the 1930s, Nguyen Ai Quoc returned to Moscow and little was heard of him. His deputies, Pham Van Dong and Vo Nguyen Giap, nurtured the seeds of revolution while other Vietnamese Communists fled to China or the Soviet Union. As Quoc himself had stressed, timing was essential because, lacking arms and strength of numbers, the revolutionaries could succeed only by taking advantage of favorable circumstances.

In the 1930s, women were specifically recruited for the resistance. The Communist Party platform of 1930 stated that they must be freed from "bourgeois ideas, . . . enabl[ing] women to participate in the revolutionary struggles of the workers and peasants. . . . If women do not take part in these struggles, they can never emancipate themselves." The program of action called on the Party to give women workers and peasants "intensive political education, arouse their class consciousness and enable them to join the organization of the working class." The authors bemoaned the fact that women and peasants were slow to join the movement because they were afraid of retaliation and full of "feudal ideology," but proper education could arouse them from their normal lethargy, excessive modesty, and resignation. The platform called for a women's commission to be formed at all levels in the Party and for peasants and women workers to be recruited in the trade unions. At this time, the Association of Women for Emancipation was formed. Its name was changed to the Association of Anti-Colonialist Women[43] and, in 1961, the Women's Liberation Association. Since radical women as well as men were severely punished if they were caught spreading anticolonial ideas, any proselytizing had to be done surreptitiously.[44]

The turmoil accompanying the outbreak of the Pacific War, especially the Japanese occupation of French Indochina, enabled Quoc to return to his homeland. As the Japanese moved south toward the treasure troves of Vietnamese rubber and Dutch oil, they found ready allies in the officials of Vichy France, who ruled the colony after the conquest of France by Nazi Germany. The Vietnamese Communists gambled correctly that the French would collaborate with the Japanese. When the United States entered the war, it found the main Vietnamese ally against Japan to be none other than Ho Chi Minh, who on his return from exile had taken the name by which history would know him. On his return from China, Ho and the ICP created the League for the Independence of Vietnam, or Viet Minh; the official action took place at the Eighth Plenum of the Communist Party, held at Pac Bo on the China border in May 1941. The Viet Minh was to serve as a united front against the Japanese invaders. It was a Vietnamese, as opposed to an Indochinese, group, since its goal was to cloak itself in nationalism and to hide the radical beliefs of the ICP. It immediately began guerrilla operations in Viet Bac, an area on the northern border of Vietnam, while its leader returned to China and was briefly imprisoned.[45]

Ho was released in 1943 and returned to a turbulent Vietnam. His guerrilla bands, organized by Vo Nguyen Giap, had attracted the attention of American intelligence agents operating in southern China and northern Tonkin as part of the Allied war effort. Officers of the Office of Strategic Services (OSS) met and worked with Ho in his hiding spot in Viet Bac, in hopes that the Viet Minh would help in the war against the Japanese. They assumed that Washington would support Ho's forces, since they were fighting a common enemy. American officers code-named the Deer Team met Ho himself in July 1945 when they sought his help in finding downed American fliers. Their medic, in fact, treated the seriously ill leader and perhaps saved his life. One OSS officer, Archimedes Patti, met Ho in August and helped him draft a new constitution for what he hoped would be an independent nation. Patti had occasion to remember this brief period when the United States and the Viet Minh worked together well, since he liked Ho and believed that he understood him. Later, Patti considered it a grave mistake for the United States not to have supported Ho at the war's end. To him, Ho was a nationalist, not a Communist; in their conversations, the Vietnamese leader had not revealed his ties to the Comintern. Patti realized that the Viet Minh was determined to maintain its independence even if bloodshed was the result.[46]

Women's traditional association with the home, not civic life, at first facilitated the activities of the few who were active in the Party to proselytize and act as liaisons for the Viet Minh, since they were not initially suspect. They told other peasant women of the changes in Russian women's lives under Communism, and even how they thought emancipated women lived in France and the United States. Some women went abroad to gain further instruction in Communist theory, much as Ho himself had done.[47]

As women became politically active, they, as well as men, were captured and tortured; France was determined not to lose its rich colonies in Indochina and had no reason to show particular mercy to rebel women. One of the early martyrs to the revolution was Nguyen Thi Minh Khai, who was radicalized by her father when she was still in school. She left home when her mother, fearing that she was leading a "dissolute life," forbade her from meeting supposedly disreputable men. However, her banishment gave her more freedom to work for change. She became a delegate to the Seventh Congress of the International in Moscow in 1935, and by 1940 she was an associate of Ho Chi Minh in Moscow. She returned to Vietnam the following year. But her luck ran out. Minh Khai was captured by the French and tortured, but she kept silent about Communism and anti-French activities. She died on the guillotine for her revolutionary beliefs in 1941, one of the first Communist heroines of the struggle.[48]

Other women also became revolutionaries. Nguyen Thi Nghia, from an upper-class family, took responsibility for maintaining contact between the ICP Central Committee and the Nghe Tinh region during the critical year of 1930. She was captured in December 1930 and tortured mercilessly. She attempted suicide by biting off the tip of her tongue. Although she did not die immediately, she pretended to be mute. Only when she knew that she was dying did she speak, telling her comrades to remain loyal to the Party. For a year after her death, they held seances to commune with her spirit.[49]

The men soon realized that women had great potential in the resistance. In July 1941, a group of twenty-one revolutionaries were armed and given the task of proselytizing and distributing leaflets; five of them were women. Vo Nguyen Giap, later Vietnam's most famous general, organized a group of thirty-four guerrillas, three of whom were women, in December 1944. Giap stated that the women were very useful in explaining current political developments to the villagers, who were also impressed with their ability to handle firearms.[50] Ha Thi Que, the best-known military woman of the early period, taught classes on military and political subjects for the Party in a "secure zone," an area controlled by the Party where resisters were safe from harassment by the French. She related that it was difficult to bring men to these classes because their wives thought she was stealing their husbands. A Vietnamese source stated that women constituted 20 percent of the membership of the armed units in the secure zones at this time.[51]

The women's military abilities and successes at political action fused in 1945 with the end of the Pacific War. Women participated in many of the critical events of that year.[52] They seized Japanese granaries in order to break the famine that seized the land, and in the south Nguyen Thi Dinh led a march on the administrative headquarters in Ben Tre.[53] In August, after Japan's collapse, women members of the Viet Minh joined with men to seize power in Hanoi. The leader of the Viet Minh, Ho Chi Minh, proclaimed

their victory, addressing throngs in Ba Dinh Square on September 2, 1945;
he pronounced the independence of Vietnam in words that he had learned
from the OSS, straight out of the American Declaration of Independence.[54]

Unfortunately for Ho, Vo Nguyen Giap, Truong Chinh, and Pham Van
Dong, who would be the primary players in the subsequent wars, the August Revolution was a symbolic action, not a transfer of power. The French
returned, supported by the Americans and assisted by the British and the
Nationalist Chinese. Ho's use of the words of the Declaration of Independence had not convinced the United States that he was a nationalist. To
the West, he and his followers were Communists and therefore enemies in
the new Cold War against the Soviet Union and its Communist allies. The
struggle for independence from France, the First Indochina War, broke out
within a year.

As the French war expanded, women played an increasingly large role. Ut
Tich, our opening heroine, began to fight at that time. Many other families
quietly joined the resistance forces of the Viet Minh, hiding their activities
from the French and their neighbors. Political activism was the primary
assignment of women in the resistance, and they learned how to oppose the
enemy through covert actions, liaison, and propaganda. The tasks and techniques they mastered would later be used in the war against the United
States. The Association of Anti-Colonialist Women gradually intensified its
mobilizing, recruiting, and indoctrinating work, and its membership grew.
Although most women stayed home, passive and obedient to their fathers
and husbands, the association reached them in their villages. Those who
were involved in military action did so primarily as support staff. However,
in 1945 the first all-woman guerrilla unit was formed by Ha Thi Que, who
later became the head of the Vietnam Women's Union and a member of
the Central Committee of the Communist Party.[55]

The struggle against colonialism lasted until May 6, 1954, when the
French fortress at Dien Bien Phu, located in a remote northern valley on
the Laotian border, fell to the Viet Minh. Although the United States had
backed France with increasing amounts of money out of fear of the spread
of Communism in Asia, President Dwight Eisenhower was unwilling to come
to its aid with ground forces or atomic weapons unless Great Britain supported the United States. During the fifty-five-day springtime siege of Dien
Bien Phu, minority tribeswomen hauled goods, equipment, and ammunition on their backs from Chinese outposts to supply the resistance forces.

Dragging heavy equipment up and down steep mountains to Viet Minh fighters who were dug into the mountains surrounding the French base, they were often more reliable and hard-working than the men.[56] They carried bicycles, parts of artillery, and ammunition as well as food and weapons, and they returned the wounded to the rear. According to Vietnamese sources, two-thirds of these laborers—the *dan cong,* or civil porters—were women.[57] They were local people who could return to their villages when their duties were over.

Some women who were recruited in the struggle against France became Communist Party members, joining the People's Army of Vietnam and fighting the European and then the American enemy. One such woman was Ho Thi Bi, a colonel in the People's Army of Vietnam. In 1995, she lived in an attractive two-story house in Ho Chi Minh City. Bi, a spry but tiny woman of eighty years clad in a woolen army uniform covered with medals, related her life story in an interview.

Ho Thi Bi came from a very poor family that lived near Cu Chi, a rural district near Saigon; her mother was a widow with three children to raise. Bi (whose name is an adopted surname given to her by Ho Chi Minh himself for her achievements) became active in the resistance as a teenager, organizing boycotts against French goods as early as 1945. As a guerrilla with the Viet Minh, she became a combatant with other peasants who fought with knives and bamboo sticks with poisoned tips. She and her comrades made up in enthusiasm and hatred what they lacked in weapons, and she fought with vigor.[58]

After the French returned to power in 1946, Ho Thi Bi, now married, took her three children to a nearby village. Since she was determined to continue the resistance, she reluctantly gave up her children to be raised by her grandmother, knowing that their crying would give away her troops' location. Leaving her children was very painful to the young mother, and she cried as she left so she might not hear their sobbing. She became even more determined to oppose the French when they attacked her village at night, raping women, stealing pigs and hens, and torturing people. She returned to Cu Chi to obtain hand grenades and was given five; she later acquired one more. She distributed the grenades to people to throw. She laughed as she remembered how the people argued over who would have the honor of standing next to Ho Chi Minh when he arrived at Cu Chi! She knew that the struggle would be long and brutal. Her small force did manage to kill six French soldiers and destroy one artillery piece in the ensuing battle.

Ho Thi Bi recalled that after this battle, General Tran Van Tra of the People's Liberation Armed Forces learned of her heroism and asked to meet her. He gave her a pistol and ordered her to organize a guerrilla division. She lent the weapon to each person in her unit in turn; that fighter then had five days to acquire one for him- or herself. Many fought with fake guns carved from wood until they got a weapon of their own. They were quite successful against the French and later the Americans. Cu Chi was a major base of revolutionary activity in the American war and the center of a 200-mile complex of tunnels used by the guerrillas. During the wars, Ho Thi Bi supplied weapons, food, and clothing to the combatants.

To break Ho Thi Bi's will, the enemy captured and killed her husband and her younger brother, and at the same time her youngest child died. She described the pain she felt at the deaths of the "dearest people to her." But still she had to "obey Uncle Ho since she knew she was a daughter of the Vietnamese nation and had a duty to obey the nation's tasks, written on her back." Revenge became a motivation for her, as it did for so many others.

The French put a price on her head; her picture was posted everywhere, but the people hid her. After the French surrendered at Dien Bien Phu, Bi was ordered to arm and provision a support division of southern Party members who went north after the Geneva Accords. During the American war, her work was in provisioning troops, and she was primarily stationed in the North. She finally returned to Cu Chi, and then was ordered north again to prepare for the campaign to liberate the South. By the time she returned to the South, victory had been won. She considered the three most important events of her life to be witnessing the August Revolution in 1945, joining the liberation army to retake Hanoi, and witnessing liberation day in South Vietnam. She also witnessed the liberation of Kampuchea in 1978. She knew Ho Chi Minh, lived at his home in Hanoi for three days, and was "adopted" by him. As her career progressed, she received many awards. She became a Heroic Mother, Hero of the People, and Hero of the People's Liberation Armed Forces. Le Thi Nham Tuyet, distinguished professor of anthropology at the University of Hanoi, noted that the enemy themselves named Ho Thi Bi, a Cu Chi guerrilla, "heroine of the eastern zone."[59] The walls of her home were covered with pictures of her activities, especially times when she was with Ho Chi Minh. Although in 1995 she was quite frail, she went to her office each morning and worked for the veterans' association, but in the afternoon she devoted herself to her flowers. As we parted, Bi clung to me and gave me one of her many medals, inscribed with a picture of Lenin.

Interviews with Ho Thi Bi and other women prompt a slight digression on the nature of oral history, such as I conducted with her. In Jan Vansina's analysis, the subject of the interview searches for the "principles of selection which link individual reminiscences and [attempts] . . . to evaluate their impact on each reminiscence." These generally involve dialogues with significant others and include hearsay along with eyewitness accounts.[60] Colonel Bi's account involved all of these things. She was elderly and a hero besides, and clearly the subject of many interviews. Since she was a loyal Party member who had distinguished herself in combat as well as logistics, her words went unquestioned even when the chronology and dates were not clear. As I talked with her, a secretary took notes for a story in the veterans' newspaper, not for fear of what this well-rehearsed woman might say, but for the importance of her audience—me. Although Bi repeated herself and spoke so quickly that my interpreter was unable to catch all that she said, her words were intended to be taken as literal truth. To one unfamiliar with the political context in which she spoke, her story was significant on several levels. First, she was one of the few living "heroes" whose title had more to do with what she had done than what she had lost. Second, for purposes of this book, she was most active during the French war and was able to narrate people's feelings (insofar as she knew them) during that period. But she also demonstrated the continuity between the war of resistance against France and the war against America and its South Vietnamese "puppets." Finally, the warmth with which she greeted me indicated a willingness to bond with another woman, which the Women's Union itself exemplifies.

Although women continued to participate in military aspects of the conflict against the French, they were certainly not men's equals. They did engage in combat, and in 1952, according to figures that are somewhat suspect, 840,000 female guerrillas operated in the North, while two years earlier, 140,000 had fought in the South.[61] They also made remarkable achievements at acquiring a rudimentary level of literacy, primarily through the efforts of the Women's Liberation Association. By 1949, 70 percent of the women in the free zones (liberated from colonial rule) could read and write, working during the day and studying at night.[62] Women in the Party had acquired an independence that freed their husbands to go to war: they were not a burden, but an asset as sisters in the resistance.

But some old traditions persisted. Polygamy was not outlawed until 1958, and the law against it was difficult to enforce. Standards of living and health were probably no better than they had been before the French departed. Women who were from families that supported the French or who were Roman Catholic, lived traditional lives, unlike the revolutionaries, and they observed roles appropriate for Vietnamese womanhood far different from those of the radicals.

The execution of Nguyen Thi Minh Khai demonstrated that penalties for opposing colonial rule applied to women as well as men, as did the execution of Vo Thi Sau, only sixteen years old, who was executed in 1952 for having killed two French soldiers. Today a martyr memorialized by a large new statue on Con Son, her memory is dramatized for visitors.[63] Aside from such stories of heroism and martyrdom, revolutionary women's most singular achievement during the French war was probably at the battle of Dien Bien Phu—where they demonstrated their talents for logistical support.

Some 1 million women had participated in the anti-French resistance.[64] For many revolutionary families, the experiences of that war only foreshadowed those of the next. The war was concluded by agreements signed in Geneva, Switzerland, in June 1954. France, with the concurrence of China but not the United States, agreed to withdraw from Indochina within two years. Laos and Cambodia were to be independent. The Viet Minh guerrillas occupied large parts of Vietnam, yet Ho Chi Minh's allies, China and the Soviet Union, did not want him to become too strong. Thus after much debate, it was decided to divide Vietnam provisionally at the seventeenth parallel, pending elections in two years to select a government for the whole independent nation. This line was not to be considered a political boundary. In the meantime, the northern Democratic Republic of Vietnam could continue its Communist-led government, while the southern portion, renamed the Republic of Vietnam, would be ruled in parliamentary fashion by a new regime headed by President Ngo Dinh Diem, a Catholic from Annam who had returned from long years in exile. The Viet Minh forces were to depart from the South, and no foreign troops or arms were to be added to the North or South as the French withdrew. Everyone would be free to decide in which zone he or she wished to live; for 300 days, the populations could relocate without reprisal.[65] But this last provision remained murky, for many Communists were "stay-behinds," who remained covertly in the South but were loyal to Ho Chi Minh. Catholics who lived in the North did move to the South, and gradually the French withdrew.

Luong Thi Trang, whose prison stories were discussed earlier, typified the stay-behinds. In 1995, she was sixty-four years old, one of eight children born to a revolutionary family. All her siblings had been revolutionaries and Party members. Five had fought in the French war; one died in 1954. Four of her brothers had been sent north in the regrouping, but Trang was ordered by the Party to be a stay-behind, remaining in Ben Tre and working covertly with other Party members to promote revolution. She took part in demonstrations, proselytized, and worked in the Women's Liberation Association to support women's rights, win converts, and aid the revolution. Her sisters worked and then married, staying in or near Ben Tre. Many of her family members died in the American war. As that war expanded, Trang became a courier for the revolutionary leader Nguyen Thi Dinh, but was arrested in January 1959 by Ngo Dinh Diem's forces. A prized captive for the southern regime, she could provide it with a wealth of information on Communist activities if her will could be broken. She was sent to all the major prisons in the South—Thu Duc, Tan Hiep, Con Thien, and finally Con Dao. Despite being brutally tortured, she revealed nothing. She was beaten heavily, but survived despite minimal rations and little water. She was not released from Con Dao until 1973, more dead than alive.[66]

Many other women soon joined what was to them not just a war, but a revolution. Two sisters, impressive nationalist women leaders, Co Bac and Co Giang, the latter the wife of a leader of the Vietnamese Nationalist Party (VNQDD), were guillotined for their advocacy of a strong role for women. Their deaths in 1960 made them martyrs in both North and South, and they were honored by Communists as well as nationalists, although they were not Party members.[67] Women were recruited on the basis of the Party's gender-equality rule, yet the top leaders were male.[68] The French war was a prelude to the next phase of social and military conflict in Vietnam, which would demonstrate beyond doubt women's capabilities in wartime.

2

. . . .

WAR IN THE DELTA,
WAR IN THE JUNGLES

As France prepared to leave Vietnam, the staunchly anti-Communist Americans appeared. Washington knew little about Vietnam's history and traditions, and saw in Ho Chi Minh just another Communist enemy, a front for an expansionist China. Although the United States had paid up to 80 percent of the costs of the French war in Indochina, it had failed to keep the French in the field against the forces of Vo Nguyen Giap. The administration of President Dwight Eisenhower now put its efforts into constructing the Southeast Asia Treaty Organization (SEATO), a bulwark against Communist expansion and an umbrella over Indochina, which was prohibited by the terms of the Geneva Accords from joining foreign treaties. The United States was determined to back the new anti-Communist regime that it had helped install in Saigon, led by the returned Catholic mandarin Ngo Dinh Diem.

The Geneva Accords gave people in Vietnam the right to live where they wished. For 300 days, a huge movement took place—not an equal movement, but an exodus from the North to the South. Northern Catholics, frightened about their right to practice their religion (and stimulated to leave by American covert propaganda), moved south, while southern Communists moved north. But most "undetected" Communists were ordered to stay behind in the South, to foment any future "political" struggle or even armed uprising if the promised election for a national government did not take place. Whether Hanoi believed in the guarantee remains debatable, but by 1956 it was clear that no voting would take place. Diem, supported by the Americans, opposed the election, fearing the real likelihood of a victory by the charismatic and well-known Ho Chi Minh. Many Americans also doubted that the Communists would in fact allow free elections—defined by Western standards. By 1957, American military personnel had begun to replace French military advisers and to train and advise soldiers of the Army of the Republic of Vietnam (ARVN). These soldiers and an even harsher adversary, the ruthless Saigon police, headed by Dr. Tran Kim Tuyen, began to arrest and kill opponents of the new regime. They especially sought out the "stay-behinds," the core of the Viet Minh in the South. Diem christened this group of revolutionaries the Viet Cong—that is, Vietnamese Communists, with a pejorative connotation—and for the Americans the name stuck. Although many of the Viet Minh consisted of nationalists who wanted an end to foreign domination, the Americans accepted Diem's classification of all his political opponents as Communists.

Although the United States had supported French opposition to the Viet Minh throughout the First Indochina War, President Eisenhower had resisted the use of American troops. The first American soldiers who entered South Vietnam in 1957 were officially advisers, to train and support the ARVN in the same numbers as the withdrawing French advisers.[1] Although the United States had not signed the Geneva Accords, it did not intend to violate them openly—thus the restriction on numbers. But the containment policy gripped Washington; the United States intended to create a strong independent state in the South to counter the Communist regime of the North. Meanwhile, Ho Chi Minh wished to avoid direct confrontation with the United States until his regime had built a socialist economy; the Communist Party had to consolidate its hold over the North and reform land ownership. Ho did send some limited aid to the former Viet Minh in the South. It traveled by sea or down a braid of trails that ran through the Truong Son Mountains and that the Americans later labeled the "Ho Chi Minh Trail." Extensive supplies and regular troops from the People's Army of

Vietnam (PAVN) began to infiltrate the South in May 1959, after the decision in January of the Fifteenth Plenum of the Communist Party to unify the North and South by force.[2] Conflict already had occurred with the arrival of American advisers in 1957 and the introduction of northern troops in the South.

Women in the Democratic Republic of Vietnam and the Republic of Vietnam were affected in diverse ways by the armed conflict with the United States and the ARVN. Since the First Indochina War had taken place mostly in the North, the women there soon learned the Viet Minh's slogan: "All people for the Resistance." Their experiences with war consisted of undertaking a wide range of activities, providing "all for the forefront" support, as they called it. When the bombing began, they had to help their families and the land to survive. In the South, those women whose men fought for the Saigon government faced a different future. Some young women were recruited by Madame Ngo Dinh Nhu (Tran Le Xuan), the president's sister-in-law, who formed a women's military unit to march and train as the men did; a few even learned to fire pistols. However, few Saigonese were attracted to her cause, which was highly puritanical and mainly for show.

In many ways, the cause of resistance was more appealing than that of the French-educated Catholic elite who ruled the South and their American advisers. The thread of revolution in the South was long-standing, and many of those who followed it were converts to Communism or descendants of those who had expelled the French. Resistance deepened, especially in the countryside from where many young pro-Communist fighters had departed for the North. Peace, the promised elections, and unification did not come, and male and female Communists faced a struggle that soon became one of sheer survival and raw determination, as the police and army determined to eradicate them.

Whether women's efforts required a radical change from the traditional Confucian three obediences and four virtues remains moot. The peasantry felt that Diem's pacifying civil guard threatened their lives. Many peasant villages were suspiciously lacking in men, while guerrillas shot at government troops and American advisers. If women were compelled to fight by the presence of foreign invaders, people responded with another saying: "If the country is invaded by the enemy, the family will be destroyed." The image of the fighting woman struggling to save her family and the fatherland was a familiar one.[3] The idea that "even women would have to fight" was a call for women to fight back, to become involved, justifying their actions in terms of a tradition of resistance. Although the slogan did not necessarily mean that women should become Communists, this is the interpretation that the Communist regime, and particularly the Vietnam Women's Union, stresses today, decades after the war.

In the South, the situation was more fluid than in the North: there was no front line, areas held by the resistance changed hands many times, and even Saigon was not safe from Communist terrorism. Since American military forces had been ordered by General William Westmoreland, commander in chief of the American forces in South Vietnam, to follow a "body count" strategy as the determination of victory—wearing down the enemy by attrition rather than taking and holding territory—the entire southern countryside was transformed into hostile territory, with its people as enemies, women and children as well as men. Even non-Communists had no choice, as they saw it, but to resist by all means available.[4]

The resistance in the South was formally organized on December 20, 1960, as the National Front for the Liberation of Vietnam (National Liberation Front, or NLF); its formation was not announced by Hanoi until January 29, 1961. Its program demanded the ouster of the Diem regime, a national assembly based on universal suffrage, and a government that included all people, parties, religious groups, and wide-ranging reforms. The Americans were to leave, the property of their "stooges" was to be confiscated, but with leniency toward those who had accepted the regime passively. Reunification with the North would come much later. The NLF at this early stage included former Viet Minh, followers of the Cao Dai and Hoa Hao religious sects, members of minority ethnic groups, idealistic students, farmers from the Mekong Delta, and refugees of many kinds from the Diem regime; it was, despite this diverse membership, an organization through which the Lao Dong, or Worker's Party—the Communists—could work. Among the founders were two women: Nguyen Thi Dinh and Duong Quynh Hoa.[5] The NLF formally organized an army, the People's Liberation Armed Forces (PLAF), in February 1961. Its goal was not the violent overthrow of the Diem regime, but a coalition government in which the Communists eventually would dominate: the weakening of the Saigon regime bit by bit and its gradual usurpation by opposition forces. The members of the NLF were to engage in agitprop, the Communist word for propaganda, promoting their cause, winning recruits, and eluding capture by the ARVN or Saigon police or Americans.

For those who joined the National Liberation Front and the Women's Liberation Association, endless struggle became a way of life. The Communist way of war was based on continual struggle until absolute victory was won. The basic concept was *dau tranh: dich van,* or political action among the enemy (the supporters of the Diem and the Saigon regimes); *binh van,* or political action among the soldiers of the ARVN; and *dan van,* political action among the people.[6] Which type of struggle should take place depended on specific circumstance, since military action should never be undertaken unless the odds were clearly in the Front's favor. All orders came from the Party and the cadre who advised the local guerrillas: the system ran from the top down. Regardless of whether military struggle was to be undertaken, political struggle continued—to maintain morale, to win new recruits, to discourage Vietnamese soldiers from fighting for the Republic, and to harass government officials with complaints and demands about the damage done by American high-tech warfare. For these tasks, women were ideal, particularly after 1965 when a shortage of soldiers forced the Front to utilize them not only as proselytizers but also occasionally as fighters.[7] Hence a discussion of the women's organizations at city, village, and hamlet level will help explain the diversity of women's tasks, the expectations placed on them, and their relationship to the Communist Party.

According to a diagram drawn up by American military officials based on captured enemy documents, mass associations occupied a role at every level in the Party structure.[8] At the top, the Party Central Committee in Hanoi gave the orders, and the Central Office of South Vietnam (COSVN) carried them out in the South. Although the Americans envisaged COSVN as some sort of South Vietnamese Pentagon, it was in fact a group of political and military leaders with no fixed location who transmitted orders but did not have as tight a connection with Hanoi as the United States presumed. There were Party committees at the regional, provincial, district, and village/hamlet levels. Although so-called liberation associations or mass organizations presumably existed for every group in society from Buddhist monks to artists, in fact the most important were the Worker's Liberation Association, the Farmer's Liberation Association, the Youth Liberation Association, and the Women's Liberation Association.[9] The women's organization replaced the patriarchal family as the primary affiliation group because men were often away at war. Women had what was referred to as a three-pronged task. First, they were to do military work in a variety of ways: they acted as liaisons between village and jungle and performed intelligence work; they provided food and clothing for soldiers, hid them from the enemy, and nursed the wounded and sick; and they recruited other women as well as men for the Front. Second, they were to conduct "face-to-face" struggles, demonstrations against enemy troops and the government in which they harassed ARVN and American soldiers, interfered with troop movements, and badgered government officials. Third, they covertly distributed propaganda leaflets where the enemy could find them, urging their opponents to "come over" to the side of the revolution.[10] On occasion, they fought with the militia or guerrillas, a task considered outside the "three-pronged" assignment because it was possible for only a few. Women also assumed political roles, becoming cadres and rising in administrative ranks. More than 30 percent of the NLF cadres were women, and they held more than 30 percent of the positions on district- and provincial-level committees.[11] In Yen Bay Province, women made up 50 percent of the cadres, according to various articles in the NLF publication, *South Vietnam in Struggle*. (The percentages stated were always approximate and since they usually came from sources very sympathetic to the Communist cause, they cannot be considered reliable; they also changed over time.)

Women of all ages participated. Teenage girls dropped leaflets, infiltrated the ranks of Saigon's soldiers to persuade them to return to their home villages and join the Front, and encouraged families to support the revolution by paying taxes and giving soldiers rice, hiding places, and aid. Nguyen Thi Dinh, who would become the most important long-haired warrior in the South, began her revolutionary career by dropping leaflets. "Face-to-face" struggles involved more direct action: women in groups demanded of a village leader or military commander compensation for their dead, for the loss of crops and livestock, and for the destruction done by chemical defoliants. By yelling, banging drums and wooden fish, and besieging the soldiers, they created mass disruption. Women also set up road blocks, dug booby traps, and called strikes in factories and markets. In several instances, women held their children in their arms and lay down in the middle of a road to prevent enemy armored cars from passing by and destroying their rice crops and fruit trees. One report stated that the women in a township in Long An Province held picks and hoes and stood in front of enemy tanks to prevent them from destroying the rice fields.[12] But they also risked being beaten and arrested for such activities.

Women of the resistance cited cruelty by South Vietnamese and American troops as further justification for revolt. In 1965, a procession of women in the My Tho area marched on troops and police: they were led by a sixteen-year-old girl, Truong Thi Bay, who carried a banner. When police shot her dead, her place was immediately taken by eighteen-year-old Nguyen Thi Be, who also was mortally wounded. Then a third young girl took the lead and was killed. But when the demonstrators continued to surge forward, the soldiers finally lowered their weapons.[13] Such episodes composed the folklore of revolution: the women became martyrs, and their actions were held up for emulation at countless meetings of the women's association throughout the South.

Masses of women who undertook such demonstrations did not spring up independently; they had to be carefully organized so that the "crowd psychology" would encourage other normally passive villagers to join the dissenters. The element of terror—the fear not only of government soldiers and police, but of the National Liberation Front itself, which carried out planned or random assassinations of its opponents—had to be overcome. One such action was the "Quach Thi Trang" incident in 1963, when a sixteen-year-old student was killed by Diem's riot police in a melee; she became the first martyr of that year. A statue in her memory was erected outside the Ben Thanh market in Saigon. Women who hesitated to join demonstrations might be ostracized by their neighbors or subjected to serious pressure. Once a group was assembled, it could be directed to act in many ways to disrupt government activities and promote the NLF's cause.

At first, women were not involved in the military struggle, in part because they lacked weapons and training. Even when they had weapons, the Front could not waste ammunition to train them in its use. Some practiced with wooden rifles, while others were encouraged to find weapons on the battlefield. They might use wooden guns to scare soldiers, but few women participated in battles. As the story of Ut Tich demonstrates, teenage girls were the most likely prospective warriors. Most women, tied to their home village by family obligations, were more effective in other ways, such as taking part in face-to-face demonstrations and propagandizing for the Front. In one account of village-level activity, in 1957 a young recruit, Ta Thi Kieu, wanted to take military action against particularly villainous local officials who had abused fellow villagers and members of her own family, so she led a large demonstration against them. She was forbidden by Party leaders to attack the few soldiers left at the nearby base, even though all her guerrillas were armed with poles. She was chastised by the local Party secretary, who reminded her that the struggle was political. "You always think of armed struggle only," he said.[14] She later became an army officer and was awarded the title Hero of the People's Liberation Armed Forces. The young were enthusiastic and fearless, and as the war intensified with the arrival of American ground forces, the Front recruited irrespective of gender. Ta Thi Kieu was admonished for wanting to fight, but at this early stage, Hanoi discouraged fighting back: the Communists were not yet ready to take on the United States.

The political struggle was key to the Front's success. Female cadres spent months with villagers, carrying out *dan van* propaganda activities, such as teaching politics and stirring up hatred of local officials for their tax-collecting methods, their torture and imprisonment of those suspected to be Communist, and their drafting of young men into the ARVN—in sum, for their denying the dignity of the masses and coercing them into war. This was not easy work. Not all peasant women approved of the way the NLF women had become involved in political activities—they talked "manly talk," which dealt with fighting, struggle, and politics, not home and children. The activists lived with male cadres, and they used jargon that the average peasant did not understand. However, the cadres were persistent.[15]

The leaders organized meetings, sending messages by couriers to marketplaces, where women normally gathered to sell or trade their goods. It was easy to start demonstrations at the markets: the women were there daily, and their tasks, however menial, were essential to the economic survival of the countryside. At markets, intelligence easily could be communicated by liaisons to the Front. Market women had been recruited earlier by the Women's Liberation Associations in their hamlets and villages, and all they needed was a cause, a specific incident to spark an outburst, provided they had proper leadership. The bombing of a village, death of their kin, or defoliation of their crops was often a sufficient cause.

The critical role of the Communist Party in the Women's Liberation Association was often hidden. A document captured by the Marine Corps First Division on February 15, 1967, elaborated on the Party tasks for that year. The major item stressed was the importance of ideology. Even the illiterate were to be taught Marxism-Leninism and the writings of Ho Chi Minh so that all would know what it meant to be a Communist. The cadres were to be trained and improved. The document stressed recruiting people from the peasants' and workers' class and teaching them to be aware of their class interests—a clear appeal to basic Marxist tenets of class struggle. Where many female Party members already existed, the cadres were instructed that "it is necessary to select one or two comrades and introduce them into the chapter committee." This would involve their moving up the ladder of responsibility, to village, district, or provincial level. The goal was to strengthen Party cells to carry out plans developed by the Party. If a cadre could operate openly because he or she possessed Saigon identification papers, the selected person had to be capable of leadership.[16]

The document also emphasized the importance of secrecy in the Party, concealing the identity of those who were members, especially new recruits. The author warned of the need to reconsider the total who operated underground, particularly the number of female Party members who "stay[ed] close to the people and identif[ied] themselves with the people in order to lead the people."[17] In the previous year, the writer noted, the development of the Party had been very slow, especially in so-called weak areas and among women. This document was only one of many that urged the enlistment of more women, especially the young. Village cadres, female cadres, and ethnic minorities needed to be recruited, but Party members were warned not to "underestimate and wrongly evaluate female cadre and ethnic minority cadre or demand too much from them." Yet it was essential to train people, especially the young, to replace male cadres in certain tasks, which were not enumerated.[18] Usually women would work in the village, since they made excellent home guards as well as militia members and could tend crops, hide food and guerrillas, and proselytize, but the young could leave the village and work with the NLF in the jungle or mountains.

Women did not have to be Party members to work with the women's associations. The Communist Party was always an elitist organization, emphasizing quality rather than quantity. Only when the military situation was grim and casualties were high did the Party recruit to replenish numbers and not discriminate to bring in committed ideologues; further indoctrination could come later. But women—young girls or old women—would hear the same message as Party members: hate the enemy, drive out the foreign aggressors, protect and save the fatherland. They were propagandized about their servile position under the "feudal" French regime—despised, ill-treated, subject to abuse in their own homes. The regime of Ngo Dinh Diem was no better, for despite its Catholic morality, its soldiers debauched and violated women and tortured and imprisoned them. The fact that Diem did not outlaw polygamy until 1958 provided potent propaganda for women, as did the behavior of his police and the treatment of women in prisons. As the number of Americans in the country increased, their deleterious effects on life in Saigon, particularly the way in which they treated bar girls, prostitutes, and the general population, was publicized by the Women's Association. Peasants were reminded that the Americans had turned the capital city into a giant whorehouse. The propaganda of the Women's Liberation Association stressed the inequality of women under the old regime and its continuation under the Diem–America government, as the group called it, and promised that they would be equal in every sense when independence was won.[19]

In villages that were secure, as well as those contested between the Front and the government of Vietnam (GVN) or actually under Party control, indoctrination sessions took place at night. Leaders taught slogans, emphasized goals, and stressed the NLF's achievements. The Party developed lists such as the "four goods" and the "three virtues" to guide women in their duties. If they became negligent, they had to engage in self-criticism and then were harshly chastised by village Front members. Self-criticism was a highly important tool in Communist ideology, since it forced adherents to constantly scrutinize themselves as well as one another for signs of deviation or backsliding. In that way, everyone could be kept in line, morale raised, and determination for victory kindled even in the face of setbacks and defeats.

Despite its need to recruit, the Party cautioned against taking in too many members, over whom it might lose control. "Opportunism" or "voluntarism," allowing the group to move the way its members wanted, rather than following instructions from the Party, was to be avoided, but Women's Associations tended to operate that way. Hence the Party warned the Women's Liberation Association that only 20 percent of those who showed up in a "general struggle" or demonstration should be considered for membership. In this manner, the "hard-core" essence would be preserved, while the larger numbers could be rallied when a mass demonstration against Saigon soldiers, government officials, or even American bases was organized. The rank and file were urged to support the revolution because it was morally the right thing to do. According to one Party document, the women were to practice the "five loves: love of country, love of work, love of equality, love of the masses, and love of peace." They were to struggle unceasingly, but without tangible reward. In Douglas Pike's pithy phrase, women were indeed the "water buffalo of the Revolution."[20]

The years 1960 and 1961 were landmarks in the history of the revolution because of two events: women's uprisings in Ben Tre Province, and the formation of the National Liberation Front. The founding of the NLF became the basis for endless arguments among historians over whether the war in the South was a spontaneous uprising by beleaguered peasants abused by the cruel regime of Ngo Dinh Diem, or a Communist movement headed by well-trained cadres that took its orders from Moscow, Beijing, and Hanoi. It was a continuation of the Viet Minh and, like its predecessor, included left-leaning students, intellectuals, religious groups, and Party members; its direction did come from Hanoi. Hanoi and the Communist Party set the guidelines and gave the orders for the military struggle in the South, operating through COSVN.[21] But the events in Ben Tre indicated the spontaneous nature of some of the upheavals, which came in response to provocations by Saigon's troops.

The Ben Tre uprisings, or *dong khoi,* were led by one young woman, Nguyen Thi Dinh, whose career in the National Liberation Front and later as president of the Vietnam Women's Union would give her respect among women, although during the war she was virtually unknown. Years later, she recorded her early life in a memoir for her people and a testimony to the strength of Communism in the Mekong Delta. Dinh resided in a province known ever since the French colonial period for its revolutionary tradition.[22] Remote and isolated, it had a long history of uprisings against oppressors, including one in the 1920s, in which the Thanh Nien movement, which was the nucleus of the future Communist Party, challenged the French.[23] Another uprising, the Nam Ky, took place in Ben Tre in 1940.[24] The area also had close ties to the Communists in the North; General Secretary Le Duan was sent in 1957 to lead the revolution in the South. He lived in a peasant's home, hiding in a false-bottomed cupboard.[25] After the Geneva Accords in 1954, the Diem government selected this province as one of six Communist strongholds to be purged of the radicals, who were to be forced to the North. But the ARVN missed some, while other peasants were radicalized when land distributed to them by the Viet Minh from the rich peasants was seized and given back to the wealthy.

Dinh, who was born in 1920, joined her brothers in the war against the French at age fifteen. Under their direction, she began dropping leaflets prepared by the Party and was herself radicalized. A friend of her brothers asked for her hand, and she enthusiastically concurred in her father's acceptance; she loved him and his politics as well. She became pregnant a few months after their marriage, but three days after the birth of their son, her husband was arrested. She was able to see him in prison only once. He was sentenced to five years in Poulo Condore, the French name of the prison on Con Son, and then would be exiled to another French colony for five years. When she learned that she, too, was to be arrested, she gave her son to her mother to raise and actively joined the revolution. Prison made her more radical, and her fellow prisoners gave her pointers in tactics: they soon killed a French guard. In 1943, she was returned to her native village and put under house arrest because of ill health. She then learned that her husband had died in prison. For the rest of her life, she resolved to avenge his death.[26]

Dinh then began to work radicalizing women for the Women's Liberation Association and the Communist Party. The Province Party Committee ordered her to strengthen the women's organizational network, and at the end of 1945 she was elected to the Executive Committee of the Women's Liberation Association. When the committee members visited a unit that had returned from combat, they saw for themselves how short the supply of arms was. Dinh was then instructed to travel to the North, report to Ho Chi Minh, and ask for arms for resistance in the South. This meant persuading him to reverse the policy of focusing on the North at the expense of revolution in the South. But she and others were convinced that without northern aid, the Viet Minh would be destroyed. She and a few comrades traveled north, first by sea and then by train. When they arrived in Hanoi, Dinh learned that she had been summoned to meet Uncle Ho. He promised her the weapons she requested, only asking that the Southerners resupply themselves by taking weapons from the French troops they killed. Then he commanded that she remain in the North to attend a training class before returning home. She was overjoyed, and could only imagine how exciting it would be when Uncle Ho could visit the South.[27]

Her return to the South was very difficult, and the war itself became more heated over the next years. At one point, the Communists even lost control of Ben Tre and had to move to another province. Dinh married again, ap-

parently following Party orders.[28] She moved frequently, fighting as a guerrilla and organizing other women. Once she was traveling to a meeting of
Party district secretaries when enemy soldiers appeared. She hid in a tunnel
and buried her papers, but the soldiers found her and dragged her out. She
pleaded with them, but they appeared ready to rape and kill her. Suddenly
she saw an old woman and called to her, "Mother, I've been arrested; please
come in and ask them to release me so I can go back to my child." The
woman answered her, "What kind of a daughter are you that you didn't lis-
ten to me! I told you to stay home. Where did you go to get yourself arrested miserably like this?" The old woman then begged the commander to
let Dinh go. The soldiers still might not have done so, but they were ordered to reinforce another column under attack, so they had to release her
and leave.[29]

In January 1954, Ben Tre Province came under heavy fire, part of the
French offensives that would culminate in their defeat at Dien Bien Phu.
But this time, the Ben Tre revolutionaries were successful in defending their
land, and they resented the Geneva Accords, under which their province
reverted to Saigon's control. Dinh's son went north for further study, and
she stayed in Ben Tre. She moved constantly, since Ngo Dinh Diem's troops
had orders to bring her in, dead or alive, and she had many close calls. The
Saigon soldiers were thorough in their attempts to search out all remaining
revolutionaries, but they failed to catch her.

The situation in the delta became even more precarious when in 1959
President Diem announced the 10/59 Decree, which stated that if a cadre
was found hiding in a house, whether or not it was his, the building and all
the property of the owner would be confiscated. People were afraid to hide
the cadres, and many of them were captured, thrown into prison, sometimes
poisoned, or sometimes guillotined. Meanwhile, Dinh was transferred to Mo
Cay District, outside Ben Tre, where people were being relocated while a
strategic hamlet—a compound into which the peasants were quarantined
away from the Communists—was constructed. When Diem visited the area,
he was mobbed by angry villagers whose homes had been destroyed. Angered, he ordered that all revolutionaries in the area be eradicated. In return, Dinh and the NLF petitioned Hanoi for the right to use military force
as well as political action; the request was granted, but they were warned
that politics still came first. Besides, they still lacked weapons. The cadres
held a long meeting and decided to mount an uprising against the Saigon

soldiers: Mo Cay District, the poorest district of poverty-stricken Ben Tre Province, would be the focal point. The dates would be January 17–25, 1960, and Nguyen Thi Dinh would be in charge.[30]

The plans for the uprising were clever. Action cells were to be set up, and people armed with spears. The action began in Dinh Thuy, a tiny poverty-stricken peasant hamlet in Mo Cay District that was thoroughly radicalized. The peasants there had four rifles acquired from defeated enemy troops in the village.[31] Participants decided to make a large quantity of mock rifles out of wood and coconut to supplement the confiscated rifles; they also had a small number of mortars and the support of eighteen village committees. Despite the enemy's capture of several key comrades, who were forced to admit that a wide-scale uprising was to take place, the *Dong Khoi* in Mo Cay went as planned. The uprising was so successful that it spread, and the equipment seized was enough to equip a whole company. This victory set an example for the entire country; well-equipped troops could be defeated by radical peasants, a majority of them women.[32] The revolutionaries also identified the villagers who supported the government, so they would know whom to catch if the uprising was successful.

This success led to others and to the decision to form a military unit from Ben Tre Province. It consisted of "hard-core" youth who were dedicated revolutionaries and women who were also very strong; Dinh was chosen to represent them. Women also mounted demonstrations at which they hoisted banners demanding the resignation of Ngo Dinh Diem and his "puppet" National Assembly. Soon the uprising spread throughout the province. But the Saigon forces quickly struck back, encircling Dinh's unit. The women escaped by a clever ruse, using such homemade weapons as a "sky horse" rifle, a primitive mortar made of a pipe that fired steel pellets and glass shards dipped in snake venom.[33] They also armed the land and themselves in every way possible, copying captured weapons, sharpening bamboo in deadly points, digging tunnels, and building shelters.

Women in Ben Tre became more active in the succeeding months, and Nguyen Thi Dinh continued her rise as activist leader and Communist stalwart. After the executions of twenty guerrillas by the ARVN at the village of Phuoc Hiep, 5,000 women from six villages congregated in Mo Cay district to demand compensation for the dead and an end to the brutality of the Saigon soldiers stationed among them. Their demands were finally met, and the soldiers withdrew from the post.[34] In 1960, Dinh became active in the organization of the National Liberation Front, and three months after the formation of the NLF the Women's Liberation Association was formed. It claimed to be a direct descendent of the women's association that had been founded by Ho Chi Minh in 1930 and that had gone through many name changes.[35]

According to her editor and translator, Mai Van Elliott, Nguyen Thi Dinh closed her memoir by stating that "there was no other road to take." Elliott recalled that Dinh had told her "she would sacrifice everything for the revolution and for the interests of the masses."[36] She was clearly a committed Communist revolutionary who had extraordinary leadership abilities. She proved herself tenacious, courageous, and bold, and she paved the way for others to serve and fight as she did. Yet she realized that men resented being led by a woman, her ability notwithstanding. Interviewed years later by Don Luce of the International Voluntary Services, she was asked how she felt about not being mentioned in Neil Sheehan's book *A Bright Shining Lie,* a biography of John Paul Vann, an American military officer and civilian leader who fought in the Mekong Delta at the same time Dinh did.[37] She replied, "Oh, I understand. Men do not like to talk about women generals. Even Vietnamese men, and we have a history of famous women generals."[38]

After the war, Nguyen Thi Dinh became president of the Vietnam Women's Union and met visitors in the drawing room that once belonged to General William Westmoreland.[39] She continued her work with women until her death in 1992. A few years after her death, the people of Ben Tre erected a statue in her memory. Museums in Ben Tre, Ho Chi Minh City, and Hanoi have extensive exhibits about her, but most American accounts of the war do not even mention her, since her identity during the war remained obscure, perhaps for security. In 1982, the president of Vietnam visited Ben Tre and announced that the *dong khoi* in the province had been the "first shot" fired in the revolution in the South.[40]

The women who participated in the uprising in Dinh Thuy remembered Nguyen Thi Dinh well. Nguyen Thi Thu, an octogenarian whose wizened body showed the suffering she had undergone, related dramatically in an interview with me, "I beat the drum at the uprising." Like so many of the elderly women, she had joined the resistance during the French occupation to fight for her people's freedom. After 1954, she became active in the village Women's Association, motivating people to raise food for resistance and participating in demonstrations to stop the bombing and killing. She said that the women beat on large bamboo drums with sticks and yelled and screamed at the soldiers. They also provided the NLF forces with clothing and food. Thu made an underground pit below her house in which to hide members of the NLF. Like those of so many other women, her husband fought with the Viet Minh and then the NLF and she rarely saw him.[41]

The villagers I talked with in Dinh Thuy were motivated to join the struggle by their poverty, their hatred of the "puppet" government and its foreign sponsors, and their determination to resist its authoritarian rule. A woman who lived in Dinh Thuy described how Saigon forces burned her home; one of her sisters was killed by bombs, and a younger brother was tortured to death by the ARVN. She was captured by ARVN soldiers, who tried to burn her alive, but when the soldiers left, the other women rescued her. Some of the women were single, unable to marry during the American war because of the priority of their wartime activities and the lack of available men. By the war's end, they were too old, since their childbearing years were over. In 1995, they received a pittance from the government to help them survive, but their sisters in the Vietnam Women's Union helped them. Their needs were modest enough.

Sixty-six-year-old Nguyen Thi Sau, another villager, had been involved in the women's movement since 1945. Her mother had ten children, since she remarried when her first husband died, but only three were alive in 1975. Seven died in the American war. Thai Thi Hang, alias Ut Hong, her unmarried friend, was part of a group known as the "mother of soldiers." These women provided for soldiers who were passing through their villages by acting as surrogate mothers. Ut Hong would "adopt" a guerrilla when a particular unit was in Dinh Thuy, give him food, clean his clothes, and care for him if he was wounded.[42] If ARVN soldiers questioned her, she would say that he was a nephew returning home from a distant village and hence did not have the identification card required by the Saigon army. Such women might also claim that the men were their own sons, returning from a trip. All women who did this task shared in these duties, which were very important for the NLF.

Ut Hong provided further information about what the network of women's associations did. They spied and shared intelligence with the NLF to aid in its fight against Saigon. After a battle, they participated in the debriefing. At demonstrations, the women wore multiple shirts so they could take one off if soldiers seemed to recognize them or before they demonstrated again. This primitive disguise might save their lives. They also pulled their conical hats down over their foreheads, to hide any slogans the ARVN soldiers might have written on them. When the ARVN soldiers came the women looked for any who were originally from the province, and their wives and sisters would talk to them, urging them to defect. Ut Hong herself learned a Vietnamese martial art called *vo viet nam* and taught it to other women so they could defend themselves.

Ut Hong had been wounded three times during the war, and her age and infirmities had made her an invalid. After the war, the Women's Liberation Association had cared for her; but since the adoption of the policy of *doi moi,* the government had the funds to pay her a stipend of about $10 a month (100,000 dong).

Ca Le Du, another villager, came from a very well known family. The Ca Le family included intellectuals and teachers who became revolutionaries in 1945. When the family went to the jungle to fight the French, she and her sister were in charge of providing food, so they grew cassava, maize, and sweet potato. After the Geneva Accords, her parents regrouped to the north. She would have accompanied them, but by this time a matchmaker had arranged an engagement for her. She and her fiancé were married secretly, and they joined a special force of guerrillas in Saigon. She and her husband worked as liaisons in Ca Mau Province, the southernmost in Vietnam. She had one child and was pregnant with a second when she learned that her husband had been captured, held in a local prison, and then sent to Con Dao. She tried to care for him while he was in the local prison, but he ordered her back to Saigon, where her division would not accept her because of her pregnancy. She then returned to her village and taught other women how to fight.

But Ca Le Du returned to Saigon with her infant to protest the poisoning of thousands of prisoners at Phu Loi prison, which she said had taken place in 1959. She was arrested, and she and her infant were taken to jail. Her four-year-old child was cared for by her elderly grandparents, and being separated from him was, she said, the "hardest part of my life." She was released after seven months and returned to Ben Tre in time to participate in the 1960 uprising. Her husband also returned, and she soon had a third child, just before he left for the jungle. She was active in the women's movement in Ben Tre, but was betrayed and arrested again. When she was in prison, she learned that her father had been made ambassador from North Vietnam to Indonesia.

Ca Le Du was arrested several more times during the war. Her activities were known, as was her Party membership. The Saigon government demanded that she confess that she was a Communist, but she refused, so she remained in prison. Her husband was killed in 1970, and Saigon released her when she claimed that she had to care for her children. Her three children now live in the Mo Cay District and have Party jobs; she receives a good stipend from the government. She concluded the interview by stating a common phrase: that her actions were for her parents, husband, and children, and that her suffering had been justified.

One elderly woman of Dinh Thuy, whose mother had won the Heroic Mother award for having lost three sons in the war, was enjoined to hide guerrillas in tunnels and bunkers as her part in the struggle. She dug a hole under her pigpen and another beneath the drainage channel under the fruit trees next to her house. When the enemy attacked, she made "pig sounds" to alert the Party members so they could go underground and then move from one hole to another via a connecting tunnel. She made three pig sounds to indicate that all was clear. One man she hid was a high Party official; she put him in her own private room (probably her bunker), and only her husband knew that he was there. Signals of scratching on her door indicated that more guerrillas were coming. She planted vegetables over the entrance to the hiding place, and the ARVN could not find it. They threatened that if she did not show them where it was, they would kill her. They beat her and shot her in the side of her back, but she did not give in. She, like the others, participated in the demonstrations and the women's movement.

Other Dinh Thuy women developed these themes. One woman, who was fifty-one years old, stated in her interview that she had been ordered to find the "spies" in the revolutionary movement—in other words, counter-intelligence. She also led demonstrations in Dinh Thuy. Another woman of that generation began her revolutionary career as a teenager, placing stakes in the road to prevent the ARVN soldiers from entering the village. She also made speeches to arouse villagers against the Saigon government officials and incite them to acts of resistance. She married in 1964, but her husband was killed a few years later; she did have two children. She, like virtually all widows in Mo Cay District, refused offers of remarriage and chose widowhood as the only honorable course. To honor a husband in death was more important than in life, since that demonstrated lifelong fidelity to him. The women believed that they owed their deceased husbands more than they owed their children, since their extended family and the whole village would care for them. Widows had to continue to serve and please their mothers-in-law, a life-long duty, even though the Women's Association opposed this outmoded custom. Sixty to 70 percent of the women in this area were widows, and all had been members of the NLF.

Dinh Thuy was notable because thirty women from that village had been awarded the status of Heroic Mother for their wartime actions and their losses. Several years ago, the Association of Fighters' Mothers was created by the Party, to honor those women who had helped to house and supply troops, acted as liaison agents, and endured "ill-treatment and torture without ever revealing the hideouts of their adopted sons."[43] One woman lost her husband, her father, three brothers and sisters, and her son. She did marry again, but her second husband also was killed. That husband was a widower with a son when he married her, so the Party as of 1995 did not consider her to be a Heroic Mother. However, they were reconsidering her case, she said. The Heroic Mothers had to have lost three sons or more, so this award indicated both the intensity of fighting in this location and the determination of the resistance.

One elderly Dinh Thuy woman spoke next. Like the others, she was a veteran of the uprisings and had suffered many beatings. However, she had been very active in the conflict. She taught women how to make *punji* stakes of sharpened bamboo often dipped in feces, which they would bury in holes to trip up and disable the unwary enemy. She had lost one son to the conflict, but three of her children now worked for the Party. She considered herself lucky that her husband was still alive. They had lived through terrible times but survived, she said. Her last comment was that two months earlier the village had acquired electric power. She just wished that she had something to use it for. If only they had a television to watch for entertainment . . .

What they suffered often made radicals of the women. One woman said that she had been mobilized to join the demonstrations by the other women in the village. She, like the others, had worn two or three shirts so she could shed them and not be recognized. But she was caught and beaten, since the government thought that she was a leader of the Communist women. She was not, she insisted, but her husband was a member of the Party security force, so they were under constant scrutiny. They hid documents and letters under the family altar, but the police found them. Her husband escaped to the jungle, but she did not; she was arrested and imprisoned for three months. Her three children were cared for by the neighbors while she was away. Prison, she said, made a Communist of her. She lost two of her children in one of the many bombings that this area sustained during the war for liberation. By the end of the war, the coconut trees were gone, the rice paddies had been poisoned, and the land had been laid waste with craters and defoliants. Her land had been devastated; her family, destroyed.

Another woman, in her mid-fifties, had a similar tale—demonstrating and being beaten and teargassed, which damaged her vision. She hid guerrillas in her house, and when the Saigon troops found them, they killed her husband. She was a widow at age twenty-six, left with two small children. She then became a liaison and transported messages across the Mekong River in a nylon bag hidden under the floor of a small boat. She also participated in the women's association in her hamlet, and she adopted a child from her husband's family. Like the other widows, she affirmed her resolve to remain single. She said that she could not bear her husband's death and wanted to remain single for his memory: "I want to remain faithful to him, and I hope he will be pleased with me." She talked to him every day at the family altar, assuring him that she would remain single for the sake of their children.

That anonymous villager at least did not have to see her husband killed, as did Dan Thi Van. She described how her family was important in the National Liberation Front and often hid important people in their home. The ARVN soldiers watched her house very closely and finally sent helicopters and military forces to attack. They surrounded the house, arrested her husband and two sons, tied them to a tree, and shot them before her eyes. Another son died in 1973, fighting with the PLAF. Van spent the years after the war's end working with the Vietnam Women's Union. She decided to retire in 1995, and the Party gave its permission. She ended her interview with the comment that she could still see in her mind's eye the images of her husband and sons being tortured and killed.

In many ways, the lives of the women of Dinh Thuy, with its small dirt-floored huts with thatched roofs, typified traditional peasant lives in a poverty-stricken area of rice agriculture. It and many of the other hamlets in Mo Cay District were cut off by the Mekong River from the mainland and were accessible only by water. The women had grown up in large families and had entered marriages arranged by their fathers. They had borne many children and belonged to extended networks of kin in their village and the ones surrounding it. They paid obligations to their mothers-in-law and honored their husband's wishes, following the three obediences. They almost never married again if their husbands had been killed in the war.

Ancestor worship—honoring the family shrine and the husband's image—
was of critical importance in proving their loyalty beyond the grave. Many
of these families had maintained a tradition of resistance; their fathers and
grandfathers had opposed the French, so revolution was the logical road to
take. Since these women had been selected to talk to me, they were probably all members of the Communist Party, but the issue never came up. One
woman sought to assure me that no one in her family had ever served the
Saigon regime—that was more important. The women were active in the
Women's Liberation Association from 1960 on and in different ways even
earlier. Their wartime activities reflected traditional roles women played, yet
went beyond them. They demonstrated, yelled, beat drums and wooden fish,
carved pikes, dug pits in which to hide soldiers, made *punji* stakes, and
blocked roads so guerrillas could ambush the enemy. They propagandized
to turn the loyalties of the Saigon soldiers, and they gathered information
from them, which they passed along to the NLF infrastructure. They carried out intelligence activities, passing messages from one place to another,
and even spying on the activities of the Americans. They were captured,
beaten, raped, tortured, and imprisoned, but by their own account they did
not betray their comrades. Obviously, none who talked to me would admit
to having given in to enemy torture. (Since this area had changed hands many
times during the war, some must have gone over to the other side, either
under duress or from exhaustion.) Those who survived, in itself a feat in
this area of great violence, maintained that they did not regret what they
had suffered for the cause. They had achieved what they had fought for:
liberation and independence from foreign oppression. That they could have
had something more, something better or different, seemed never to have
entered their minds.

The *dong khoi* at Ben Tre in 1960 became famous in the annals of the war in
the Mekong Delta. Women had risen up—using voices, sticks, and drums—
to protest the war around them. They had bested the opposition's army and
added an important dimension to the widening conflict. For their achievements, Ho Chi Minh awarded them the appellation "long-haired warriors."
Eventually, with Ho's blessing, this term of approbation spread throughout
the South.[44]

3

FROM UPRISING
TO PROTRACTED WAR

In the entryway of the Women's Museum in Hanoi stands a large statue of a woman, gilded and crafted in Soviet-style realism. It is anything but typical of the diminutive Vietnamese women, but it does emphasize one point dramatically: the power of women. The statue serves as counterpart to the Communist statement regarding women's role in the new order that the revolutionaries hoped to achieve. The declaration, written in 1961, included the following words:

> Women are not only equal to men in society, they are also equal to their husbands. We will abolish inequality between husbands and wives . . . as we will abolish polygamy. . . . Family property is common property. . . . Women are equal to men in standing for elections. . . . Women must be free to choose their own professions. . . . Since they carry out the same work as men, women are to receive the same pay as men. . . . Female farmers will be allocated rice fields on the same basis as men. . . . In brief,

we plan to liberate all women to be totally free and equal in society and in their families.[1]

Peasant women—and the National Liberation Front was primarily peasant—were tied into a traditional society in which family and motherhood were preeminent. Although women who became active in the resistance might not marry, marriage was still the expectation, having children the logical outcome, and fealty to the village and the husband's family the lifelong obligation. The Party promised that it would "pay utmost attention to raising the political, cultural, and vocational standard of the women, [and] develop the Vietnamese women's tradition of heroism, dauntlessness, fidelity and ability to shoulder responsibilities." The Party also promised women workers and civil servants two months' maternity leave with full pay, before and after childbirth. This would "promulgate progressive marriage and family regulations, . . . and it would protect the rights of mothers and children."[2] Women were also recruited by promises that a new order would care for their personal needs, strengthen their traditional roles, and, indeed, free them from obligations to their mothers-in-law.

Some women who joined the Party did denounce their in-laws.[3] Others, like Nguyen Thi Dinh, actually gave their children to their parents to raise and went off to fight. But most worked for the Party in different ways, depending on their marital status, their children, and their ages. Having older children or grandparents watch young ones helped manage the woman's dual roles. The village women also hoped that their neighbors would care for their children if they were arrested, as one woman in Dinh Thuy reported had happened to her. Some tasks—such as growing and hiding rice, digging holes and concealing cadres and guerrillas, carrying messages, creating disturbances in the marketplace, and distributing propaganda leaflets—the women could accomplish and still live at home. Since women had to attend the family altar daily and produce sons to continue the family name and honor the ancestors, the activities of traditional peasant life—raising food and caring for children and in-laws—were necessary. But for dedicated Party members, obedience to Party orders began to take priority.

Female recruits were often reluctant to leave home. One female cadre explained to potential recruits that "only the Front's success could help my family and yours to overcome misery and starvation in the future."[4] But the life was hard, especially if the Front required recruits, male or female, to leave home or the vicinity of their villages. Political training was endless, conditions in the jungle were dangerous, and the rewards were distant, especially as the war escalated. Nevertheless, many did join, driven to the Front by the horrors that war brought.

Some who joined the Party did so for patriotic and ideological reasons. One woman became a member because she was angry about the way ARVN forces treated the people in her village. They extorted money from the inhabitants, she said. Another official forced a woman whose husband had regrouped to the North in 1954 to have sex with him. But when she bore him a child, he abandoned her and the infant. This angered the villagers, but they were afraid to protest because of what the troops might do to them. The final straw came when the soldiers killed the woman's father for something he had not done. At this point, another woman in the village convinced her to join the NLF, and she reported that her life became happier. She moved from her home village to another, where her job was to contact women and young girls and encourage them to join the Front. She was arrested while on a mission, but was, according to the interviewer, hired by the Rand Corporation, which was under contract to the United States Army, to interview prisoners of war and those who had defected. Throughout this time, she remained a strong believer in Communism.[5]

Another woman liaison agent told her interviewer that she believed that the Front would win, that she had joined because her village had had only a few months of freedom and peace after the Geneva Accords were signed in 1954, and that the GVN had occupied her village ever since.[6] A woman in Binh Duc hamlet, Dinh Thuy village, joined the NLF when she was very young. The proselytizer convinced her that if she joined, she would be "serving the nation and [her] own family." She was persuaded by him that the Front was the "right cause." Although he told her that the work would be easy, she found it very hard, and the Party cadre would not let her quit. She was an only child, and her mother was a widow who did not approve of her political activities. After two years, she found the courage to rejoin the Saigon forces and to inform her mother that she had done so.[7]

Other women joined the Front for diverse reasons, sometimes to outside observers quite frivolous. One woman, who rallied to the GVN in 1966, joined when a cadre promised her that if she became part of the NLF she could learn to sing and dance in the entertainment troops. The man kept urging her to enlist, and finally she did; but she missed her family and returned home when her mother found her. However, the cadre returned and resumed his appeal. The prospect of rejoining him and the twenty or twenty-five young men and women who were part of the entertainers drew her back into the Front. Soon she and he were living together, despite the Party's strictures against extramarital sex and her awareness that he was married. She told the Rand interviewer that she did not know of the man's Party activities, but realized that he had to be an important official. He finally asked her to deliver some letters; she claimed that she thought they were just routine messages ordering people to pay their taxes to the NLF, and she accepted. While she was on this mission, she was captured and went over to the GVN's side. She denied being unhappy about defecting, since she complained that the NLF had taught her only one song![8] This story had the markings of deception all over it: it sounded like the woman was attempting to convince her captors that the resistance was not really important to her, and that she did not know what was going on.

Another woman joined the NLF because it controlled her village, and she and others were frightened that they would be killed in the crossfire with the ARVN.[9] A woman who subsequently became an outstanding guerrilla in An Giang Province was recruited by the Communists, joined out of a spirit of adventure, and discovered that she had a real aptitude for killing and even took pleasure in it. Politics bored her, but in the seven years she remained with the Front, she absorbed a lot of ideology. She was made a Party member as a reward for the number of enemy troops she had killed, including three Americans.[10] In Ben Tre Province, by 1967 main force units of the People's Liberation Armed Forces had inducted two women for every one man.[11]

Women joined the NLF for reasons that stemmed from Vietnamese history, tradition, and the contemporary situation. These peasant women observed filial piety and obeyed their fathers, husbands, and sons in the traditional manner. Young women who ran away from home seem to have lacked a father figure, and their relationships with their mothers were not good. Some women followed their fathers into the NLF; others had lost brothers and fiancés to the battles or to the relentless ARVN draft. One does not read of young women defying their fathers or husbands to join the Front.

The second important consideration was the profound influence that Ho Chi Minh had among the peasants. They knew his name, they knew he was the leader of the Communist North, and they believed that following him could bring independence to their country. His picture often adorned the

family altar, and he was regarded as Bac Ho, father's older brother, an hon-
orific higher than the simple "uncle." He was the man who had led the country to victory over the French, and he symbolized independence.

Among the leaders of the Women's Liberation Association and the NLF
were urban, educated women as well as peasants. In 1965, the national chair
was Nguyen Thi Tu, listed in information the Americans collected about
the NLF as a former professor from Saigon. Vice-chairs were listed as Buu
Doan, a member of the Jarai tribe; Le Thi Lien, an NLF delegate from eastern Nambo; and Thanh Loan, an artist from Saigon. The secretary-general
of the association was Nguyen Thi Thanh, a teacher. One permanent member of the national central committee was Ma Thi Chu, a pharmacist and a
member of the Afro-Asian People's Solidarity Committee. Duong Thu
Huong was a physician, and Madame Nguyen Thi Binh was a former student when she became a leader of student protests in Saigon.[12]

The fighting intensified in late 1959 and the subsequent years, as President Ngo Dinh Diem accelerated his efforts to destroy the former Viet Minh
in the South, and the North responded by increasing aid and eventually
supporting outright combat. The NLF, formally established in 1960,
mounted powerful campaigns to recruit members for the resistance. Fearing the defeat of the GVN forces and the expansion of Communism in
Southeast Asia, the Americans sent more military advisers to the ARVN
and abandoned the pretext of keeping the total number at the same level
set for the French in the Geneva Accords. By 1963, at the end of the administration of John F. Kennedy, there were more than 16,000 American
advisers, who greatly intensified the level of fire power. Inevitably, some
of them were killed, and Americans at home became more aware of this
distant brushfire war. But the enemy remained shadowy, difficult to dis-
tinguish from the friends.

Since Hanoi feared a direct confrontation with the United States, the NLF
was instructed to avoid killing Americans in order not to draw attention to
themselves.[13] However, women were learning how to use weapons; they
drilled with wooden replicas, graduating to real weapons and bullets, and
learned other necessary skills of a guerrilla. By this time, women as well as
men were being killed in increasing numbers. From 1954 to 1965, according to one Communist Vietnamese source, female revolutionaries in the South
suffered 250,000 deaths, 40,000 disabilities as the result of torture, and 36,000

imprisonments.[14] While the accuracy of these figures is dubious,[15] the main point, that women as well as men were dying, was true. The war's severity was felt most stongly in those areas dominated by the NLF, since the Americans and the South Vietnamese were determined to destroy it.

The main goal of the Front was to increase its following, bringing in women as well as men. The Party's appeal enticed intellectuals, who could read Marxist-Leninist doctrine, but also attracted many peasants who wanted independence and peace. The Women's Liberation Association took responsibility "for the mobilization of women and for enlarging the political and social role they played in the village. . . . [T]he constant work of persuasion was the essence of the Front's political practice, and in this sense . . . it worked at the very center of the insurgents' local effort."[16]

Requirements for joining were simple: any female, over sixteen years of age and willing to cooperate in the activities of the association, was eligible. Once women entered the association, they planned activities to support the NLF organization and disrupt the GVN. Most of the tasks they did were mundane, such as secretarial work, cooking, mending clothes, and producing food. Women also served on the Village People's Revolutionary Councils, the local governmental units of the Front. One directive stated that 20 to 35 percent of the councils (which were to number between twenty-nine and thirty-five members, between the ages of twenty-one and thirty-five) should be composed of women. The order noted that "the position of chairman or deputy chairman or secretary . . . should be assigned to female personnel."[17] As the war continued, more women joined the resistance. The Vietnamese themselves attributed this to the arrival of the Americans to support the regime of Ngo Dinh Diem; women increasingly led demonstrations and marched to provincial capitals and district centers, demanding an "end to bombardment and murder, and damages to the victims."[18]

Yet early in the American war, peasant women's lack of education hampered their response to ideological training. They could not read propaganda leaflets and had little sense of political consciousness. Demonstrations against the death and destruction of one's own family and village could be orchestrated by a Party cadre, but for a peasant to become more deeply committed and actually become a Party member required learning, dedication, and loyalty. A woman guerrilla from Cambodia interviewed in the Rand study related how the Front had taught her to read;[19] many others also learned, either from the NLF directly or, more commonly, from the branches of the Women's Association in their villages.

The female cadres aroused political consciousness by reminding women about how they were exploited, unlike their sisters in the North, who enjoyed the benefits of living under a socialist regime. They educated peasant women in revolutionary action and political ideology, and they conducted refresher courses for members of village chapters during the war, providing guidance and a stimulus to action. The Party lists became the basis for training sessions. For example, the Four-Good-Quality campaign encouraged recruiting for the military, conducting political struggles, promoting farm production, and helping local residents to earn a living. The Five-Loves campaign was based on the concepts of love of country, love of work, love of equality, love of the masses, and love of peace."[20] These were all typical Communist rhetorical ideals.

The women also conducted "emulation campaigns," using as models heroines like Ut Tich and Nguyen Thi Dinh to influence ethnic minority women in mountainous areas as well as women in the lowlands, river deltas, and urban areas.[21] Emulation campaigns were standard Communist procedure; they publicized feats of heroes and intensified the conviction of their followers to mold a close-knit organization and raise soldiers' morale.[22] They promoted the three readinesses: preparedness for farming (replacing men in the fields), for sending their sons and husbands to the front, and for taking up arms themselves if necessary.[23]

According to historian William Duiker, the chapters of the Women's Liberation Association were "poorly organized and lacked militancy and a sense of direction, and their members lacked ideological commitment."[24] The documents quoted earlier indicate that at certain times and places maintaining a willingness to sacrifice was indeed a problem, but it was not restricted to women and was not continual. The ARVN certainly suffered from a lack of commitment much of the time; male and female members of the NLF also lost morale in the face of unremitting bloodshed and the terror of war. Even the Americans were not immune to such feelings as a loss of morale, homesickness, and a sense of futility stemming from ignorance about what they were fighting for. For the NLF women, the problems of organization, direction, and commitment were gradually remedied; by 1965, the NLF claimed more than 1 million women among its members, and they were an integral part of the revolution.[25] Five years later, the situation had changed; there was again a need to emphasize recruitment as well as military action, but by then the war had peaked in intensity, and many of the original participants were dead.[26]

Although all statistics are suspect, given the nature of the war and the fact that those of the NLF apply only to specific provinces at specific dates, it is clear that women were numerically important throughout the conflict. A document captured in Ninh Thuan Province in 1966 stated that there were 58 women among 367 village guerrillas, or 15.8 percent; 11,281 hamlet guerrillas, including 285 women (2.59 percent); 2,414 militia members, with 1,238 women (51.3 percent); and 159 self-defense and secret guerrillas, including 52 women (32.7 percent). Of the group, 18 percent were Party or Group members (being prepared for Party membership). The anonymous author of this NLF report noted that there had been an increase in the number of members, including women. But the Party needed more recruits from the masses, especially women, and they had to be better trained.[27]

In 1967, according to another document captured by GVN Rangers, a particular guerrilla force had been increased to 11,235 fighters, including people from villages and hamlets as well as so-called secret guerrillas. Among the total were 3,311 women, or 29 percent of all the guerrillas. There were also 850 children, 103 old men, and 250 old women.[28] As the war progressed, women increasingly participated in militia and guerrilla units. In a South Vietnamese NLF publication, probably written in 1970, the anonymous author stated that "women made up the greater part in the militia units." In several villages of district X (Phu Yen Province), for instance, "more than 50% of the guerrillas are women." The writer claimed that women guerrillas were "fighting the enemy with arms in hand" and noted that they were "organized into groups, squads, or platoons commanded by their own chiefs to fight in independent actions or coordinated with male guerrillas."[29] In one entry from a notebook captured in Binh Dinh Province, the Party secretary stated that as of March 1971, there were over 12,800 Farmer's Liberation Association members, 2,444 Youth Liberation Association members, 13,638 Women's Liberation Association members, and nearly 5,000 in the Youth Association and Assault Youth Groups in the province. (The Assault Youth Movement consisted of young people who were trained to lead guerrilla attacks against the enemy.)[30]

Although many documents indicate that the NLF was satisfied with neither the number nor the quality of its recruits, one must remember that these were guerrillas, the actual fighters of the revolution. To be a warrior required a special aptitude, and it was not always possible to screen applicants for their qualifications. An appeal in Cu Chi District in December 1966 called on the cadres to motivate "every Party member, every Group member, every

Youth, both male and female, to become 'a guerrilla.' The motivation of women to accept combat duties should be given due attention. The criterion, that one-third of the guerrillas should be women, must be reached and exceeded."[31] The anonymous female guerrilla from Cambodia said that it was common practice in her area to send recruits to an area far from their homes, so it would be impossible for them to flee.[32]

The connection between the Women's Liberation Associations and the fighting forces of the NLF was significant. The women provided all the supplies necessary to support the men at the battle sites: ammunition, food, clothing, bandages, hiding places, and the like. They had to distract the ARVN troops and subvert the activities of the government. They were to encourage and "accelerate military action," as one captured document noted.[33] The Women's Associations were the source for these battlefield support workers, and their tasks were essential to the continuation of the conflict.

The war in the South entered a new phase in 1965, when President Lyndon Johnson made the decision to send ground troops to Vietnam. He already had ordered a quick military strike in August 1964, when two PT-boats from the North had supposedly attacked two American vessels in international waters in the Gulf of Tonkin. Johnson was determined to destroy the Communist guerrillas of the South, but he waited until his reelection in November and then postponed action until the guerrillas provided provocation. Two attacks on American military advisers at Pleiku and Quy Nhon in February 1965 provided this spark, and the president retaliated with a sustained but limited bombing campaign of the North: Operation Rolling Thunder. He also obtained from Congress the Tonkin Gulf Resolution, a de facto declaration of war. The resolution gave him a free hand to respond to the so-called aggression from the North.[34] When the limited bombing did not succeed in bringing Hanoi to heel, Johnson decided to send American ground forces to Vietnam. Their first orders were to patrol the perimeters of the large air base constructed at Da Nang, protecting it from guerrilla attack so the ARVN could engage the enemy in the field. But when their presence had little effect, he sent American forces to engage in combat.

The People's Republic of China and the Soviet Union opposed Hanoi's enlarging the war by sending the PAVN south, for fear they would be drawn in to defend their ally. Hanoi conducted its own debates over expansion, but the Party concluded that the Saigon government of Nguyen Khanh, a successor to Ngo Dinh Diem, was increasingly vulnerable to collapse. The North Vietnamese also believed that the morale of the Americans was poor, as evidenced by the growing antiwar movement. Trained soldiers from the PAVN engaged in combat when the Party reached a decision that it was possible to win a victory over the GVN and the Americans within two years.[35]

After the Gulf of Tonkin incident and the beginning of the American bombing campaign, women increasingly joined the war. One woman of the resistance shouted to her comrades the apocryphal words: "Your sisters are here! Our brothers fight and we, your sisters, will support."[36] These words were uttered by "information soldiers," who mobilized others to campaign and fight, gathered data and spied on the enemy, and took up arms when needed.[37] They embodied the three readinesses that women had been instructed to follow.

Although women had many reasons to join the resistance, not all who joined persisted in their loyalty. As interviews done by the Rand Corporation for the United States Army demonstrated, women as well as men did defect. Some left the Party and the Front because they feared capture and death, others because conditions in the jungle were too onerous. Some were "brought over" by the program known as *chieu hoi*, which attempted to woo prisoners of war and potential defectors by promises that they would not be punished but would receive land and housing. Others simply concluded that the NLF would be defeated, and they wanted to join the winning side. Fear of death was a powerful motivator. Cruelty, particularly the gruesome massacre at Son My (My Lai 4), was a powerful recruiting device for the resistance, but women left the NLF when they were wounded and not cared for, when they were criticized for failing at their tasks, and when they had to spend more time with their own families (their parents, in-laws, and children) and the Party would not allow it.[38]

Another topic that caused difficulty was sex. The Communist Party advocated sexual abstinance, a difficult restriction on young men and women who were thrown together away from their families and the eyes of their home villagers. The Party's strictures came not from any particular puritanism as much as from its dedication to "first things first": one could not fight a war and carry on a romance at the same time. The NLF punished polygamy and criticized promiscuity because the latter could hurt morale. The Women's Liberation Association said that such activities demeaned women, who should remain pure for the cause. Uncle Ho's supposed celibacy provided an example to emulate for all who were not married. A reporter writing from Saigon claimed that if male and female members of the NLF were caught having sex, they could be sentenced to "3 to 10 years of confinement in the bamboo cages that serve as jail cells in remote base areas." The article, written by someone who apparently knew Party practice, stated that the penalties were becoming harsher as more women and girls joined the NLF ranks. Citing captured enemy documents, the author said, "The weak points of women are that they are credulous and cannot resist love." The Party, according to the writer, preached the doctrine of the three postponements, or *ba khoan*, to unmarried cadres: "The first is to postpone falling in love. Those who cannot resist are asked to postpone getting married. If they go ahead and marry anyway, they are asked to postpone having babies." The article was entitled, in the American slang of the day, "Vietcong Tells Girl Recruits to Make War, Not Love."[39]

Whether or not the Front went so far as to ask for the three postponements, its stated position on extramarital affairs was clear. The NLF claimed to have ended the Viet Minh custom of having women pose as prostitutes to gain access to government military posts and obtain information through "pillow talk." However, they were encouraged to tempt enemy troops and then kill them when they were close enough. Clearly, there was a fine line between being chaste and being a deadly temptress.[40] Thus in practice, the Communists were quite tolerant, since love could lead to recruitment for the Party. Indeed, had they been as rigid as these prohibitions suggest, they would have gained nothing and only alienated potential recruits.[41]

But some Party members who were caught having illicit affairs were severely criticized. Nguyen Khac Vi, alias Ba Khanh, was a prominent member of the Vietnam Alliance of National, Democratic, and Peace Forces (VANDP), a middle-class Communist front organization. Vi was caught having "friendly then sexual relations with a lady physician named Thuy serving in the Psywar [psychological warfare] Entertainment Sub Section." He was severely criticized and punished in an unspecified way for six months.[42] Other comrades caught in similar circumstances were expelled from the Party. One man, a former Party secretary of a village, had an affair with a village girl who became pregnant; he was demoted and purged, but according to the source, after he was moved to another location, he was readmitted.[43]

It was difficult, nearly impossible, to repress human nature. When single men and women met in the course of Party activities and then married, as did the woman from An Giang, that was acceptable. Although the marriage was unorthodox, in that she and her spouse spent very little time together before his death, she at least followed the accepted path for a woman, even one who was an active guerrilla. She was pregnant when she decided to defect.[44] A tale in "Fragment of a Man" reiterated the usual sexual roles. A beautiful young peasant girl met a young fighter, who returned with her to the village to warn the people of the likelihood of bombing. Along the way, Americans did begin to bomb the path, and they hid in tunnels. The emotion of the moment overcame them, and they had sex. She became pregnant and had to admit her sins to the village leader. Even though the young man was anxious to marry her, she still had to be punished: she lost her political status, was expelled from the Party, and was removed from her position as vice-chair and commander of the squad. She was also forced to leave the village.[45] She had violated Party discipline against having sex before marriage.[46]

In many cases, however, the war disrupted normal sex roles. Nguyen Thi Dinh, the general from Ben Tre, married again after her first husband died at Con Dao. Apparently, her second marriage was the result of Party pressure, so that Dinh would appear to be a "normal" and proper woman as she traveled about the countryside and worked with men. How happy the arrangement was is open to speculation: the woman from An Giang claimed to have met Dinh a second time at a reorientation session where Dinh presented her with a Colt pistol for her bravery. Dinh's husband also appeared, hoping to see his wife, but she kept him waiting for three days and three nights while she met with the women. Finally, he ran out of patience, demanded to see her, and told the provincial Party chairman that he was not acting as a Communist but as a husband. Then he "slapped his wife's face three times and declared that, from then on, they were no longer man and wife." When Dinh pronounced her dissatisfaction with him as well, they went their separate ways. When the interviewer asked the An Giang woman again if the story was true, she affirmed that it was, that she had seen the incident with her own eyes. And she sided with the husband: it was not proper for a wife to treat her husband in such a manner.[47] Given that Dinh was an exemplary military leader, one can only speculate on the meaning of the incident. Maybe she just did not like her husband and chose war rather than love, since there was no love lost in any case. The An Giang woman's reaction showed the typical response to gender roles, certainly among villagers. Wives owed certain duties to husbands, and whatever Dinh's status in the NLF, she owed her husband some respect.

The Front continually used the threat and fact of sexual abuse to lure people to its side. The Communists complained that the Americans had "attempted to turn Saigon into a brothel," a charge with much basis in fact.[48] Women and girls were warned that the Americans were engaging in psychological warfare, tempting young women and men with the crude immoral American lifestyle and exposing them to "social diseases on an unprecedented scale."[49] And particularly after the massacre of over 500 people at the village of Son My (My Lai 4), the NLF had ample propaganda, based on fact, of the atrocities toward women of which the Americans were capable. One broadcast from Liberation Radio charged that the enemy was "engaging in bloody massacres," that he had struck at the women's movement using massacres and terror while "at the same time trying to mislead and seduce sisters." He also "used money and a depraved and obscene culture to persuade sisters, especially sisters in revolutionary families, to make love with him, thus undermining their family happiness."[50]

But the Americans were not the only villains. The Front charged that ARVN troops often forced women whose husbands had regrouped to the North in 1954 to divorce them and to either remarry or have illicit sex. Those who refused were considered to be Communists and were abused. They also "encouraged their henchmen to engage in love affairs with the wives, sisters and daughters of our cadre and soldiers" (with awards given to those who succeeded in doing this).[51] Liberation Radio broadcast that the ARVN troops were raping women and girls, while the GVN was charging that the Communist troops in Binh Dinh had taken hundreds of women and given them the choice of collecting taxes or promoting "soldier's morale," which turned out to be an invitation to rape.[52] The rape of women in wartime is, one might say, standard operating procedure.[53]

Variations on this theme are intriguing. Apparently North Vietnamese and South Vietnamese differed over women. According to one source, probably a defector, when South Vietnamese cadres were killed, they were being replaced by North Vietnamese (in the division with which he was familiar, the Communist Ninth). This caused problems when units that included women met the Northerners, whom the women preferred to the southern men. The southern cadres, in an attempt to discredit their rivals, told the women that the Northerners just wanted to have illegal sexual relations with them. The South Vietnamese men attempted to stir up trouble, and in many cases they succeeded; women with the Psywar Entertainment Subsection would not perform before the North Vietnamese men, who were then angered.[54]

Perhaps the most interesting anecdote regarding the behavior of a woman in the Front came from a man who had escaped from a transportation company operating in Cambodia. When he refused orders to fight, he was put in a detention camp, from which he escaped and rallied to the GVN. He reported on what he had observed while in the camp. According to his account, there was a woman in the camp named Tam Gai. She had been secretary of her Party chapter and been elected as outstanding emulator for three successive years. She had been arrested for having "chopped to death on the spot Miss Lan serving in the Hospital for having relations with her husband." Conditions in the camp were austere, foreshadowing life in the reeducation camps that would be established after Liberation. Prisoners had to work for ten to twelve hours a day, were unable to move during air raids, could not discuss their former unit's activities, were not allowed to "relate pleasure life manners [sic] in the American way," and the like. To break these laws was to risk punishment, hanging by hands and feet for a day and a night, being confined in a dark room for seven days, or being put on trial again. Gai, among others, became angered at being treated like the enemy. According to the source, she "took her vengeance on the guards, by seducing some most cruel guards and letting them have relations with her so as to denounce them and ask to transfer them from the camp."[55] Puritanical she was not.

The leaders of the Women's Liberation Association were not well known outside the NLF, and most were not known outside their own districts. Some of the long-haired warriors became famous as local heros, because they either had performed tasks worthy of emulation or had been subject to cruel and unusual punishments. Only Nguyen Thi Dinh was well known as a guerrilla, and she downplayed her role after the war, saying that men did not like to take orders from a woman and she was no different.

Several other women were prominent political leaders. Duong Quynh Hoa, a wealthy Chinese-Vietnamese woman, had been educated as a physician in Paris and radicalized by her association with Ho Chi Minh and French socialists and Communists. She returned to Vietnam in 1958 and practiced medicine in Saigon, where she specialized in providing medical care for poor children for free. She associated with other civic leaders and intellectuals who objected to Ngo Dinh Diem's authoritarian rule. They decided to form an extralegal political organization, first drawing in others who shared their goals. They also made contacts with the religious sects, the Cao Dai and the Hoa Hao, as well as the Buddhists and the few legal political parties. They did obtain support from Hanoi, although they did not think of themselves as political. Hoa was a founding member of the NLF. Although the National Liberation Front was formed in 1960, its members considered themselves to be primarily nationalists.[56]

In 1968, the dissidents created the Vietnam Alliance of National, Democratic, and Peace Forces (the equivalent of the Fatherland Front in the North), whose aim was to get the United States to leave the country. Hoa was one of the activists in this group, and the only one of its leaders to be openly affiliated with the Communists. By 1969, the NLF and the VANDP were working together, and the formation of the Provisional Revolutionary Government, or PRG (the political arm of the NLF) was an attempt to demonstrate the extensive and diverse nature of the opposition to the government of Nguyen Van Thieu. Hoa was minister of health in the PRG, and Nguyen Thi Dinh was by then deputy commander of the armed forces of the National Liberation Front. These women, together with Nguyen Thi Binh, who had risen from student activist to foreign minister in the PRG, occupied very high positions in the southern opposition, but they were not the only women in leadership roles. There were many prominent women listed in the Women's Liberation Association as well as, presumably, in NLF activities in particular areas.

In 1969, the military situation became much worse for the PRG, and the government leaders were forced to flee into the jungle. Hoa at that time was seven months pregnant. She was assisted in her escape by her husband and a bodyguard, but there was no time to pause, even though it was expected that she would have to deliver by cesarean section. She went into labor two months prematurely and gave birth to a healthy son, but he soon died from malaria.[57] She was not able to have another child.

Hoa was a wealthy intellectual and thus had several ideological strikes against her within the Party. She had spent much of her life in France, and some felt that she knew that culture better than her own. Her style of dress, her makeup, and her demand for sanitary facilities annoyed the servants in her house. Her alliance with the VANDP was an indication of that organization's attempt to appeal to a broad stratum of society, but to the United States it was just a Communist front, and Hoa's open party affiliation was more proof of that.

Nguyen Thi Dinh represented the leadership of Communist women in Ben Tre and the Delta beginning in 1960. Saigon, the sophisticated city, attracted Communist women of many sorts: Hoang Thi Khanh, a peasant from Cambodia; Nguyen Thi Binh, an educated and articulate revolutionary; and Hoa, a wealthy sophisticate attracted by its idealism. In central Vietnam, women joined through fear of the actions of the 65,000 ground forces that landed at Da Nang in 1965.

The American strategy of "search and destroy," hunting down and killing the enemy, cost many Vietnamese lives. Women in the Liberation Associations could not safely follow the three-pronged strategy of resistance that Nguyen Thi Dinh had advocated in Ben Tre. While they might be able to spread propaganda and support the NLF, harrassing the ARVN and police as well as recruiting new revolutionaries would put their lives in danger. Hanoi sent special instructions to women revolutionaries on how to resist, stressing four themes: arouse hatred among the people toward the aggressor; encourage solidarity so that the Vietnamese and the ethnic minorities would cooperate against the common enemy in the war; use revolutionary violence, including assassination and terrorism; and believe and preach the inevitable victory of the Party and the revolution.[58]

Women had special duties in this area, with its heavy concentration of American, ARVN, and South Korean forces. They had to fight and bring supplies to the battlefield, continue propaganda and recruitment, care for children, and work at all levels in the Party since the men had been recruited as guerrillas by the NLF. The fighting was intense in the countryside, so the Women's Liberation Associations had to teach peasants basic gestures of submission and simple English phrases (such as "don't shoot" and "me not VC") to try to protect themselves from death. Whenever possible, however, women were to use revolutionary violence to kill Americans. They were armed with Russian weapons and taught to use them.[59]

In Da Nang itself, the opportunities to resist were limited by the presence of the Americans and South Vietnamese. Yet for seventy-six days in 1966, the women brought the city to a standstill when they encouraged all workers to go on strike. They shut down the markets, closed the schools, and spread revolutionary doctrine. But from this point on, the war became harsher: the Communist-controlled liberated zones were eradicated; the so-called white areas, which had been defoliated around bases, were increased in size; and the women could no longer use political and revolutionary resistance. Instead, they were taught a new strategy that stressed the importance of the Party in helping people, who would then defend the land, enabling the guerrillas to kill the enemy.[60]

In the weeks before Tet, which began on January 30, 1968, the women attempted to ingratiate themselves with the Americans by bringing them candles as Christmas gifts. Their goal was to gain access to the base, but they met with limited success. They also prepared for the uprising by obtaining food and donations for the NLF. However, when the offensive began, the women in Da Nang were unable to rouse people to join the revolution; the city dwellers were unarmed, and the guerrillas were unable to establish a connection with them. The South Korean soldiers were particularly brutal in their crushing of the resistance, and American and ARVN soldiers also responded quickly. There were a few individual victories: Nguyen Thi Tam was credited with destoying four tanks, and another young woman killed many American and ARVN troops with grenades. But individual successes by these fighters were not enough.[61] The general uprising failed, as it did throughout the South.

The leaders of the opposition acquired a certain notoriety in Vietnamese society. The vast majority of women involved in the Front were anonymous, but the fact that they were revolutionaries, that they fought the government, was unusual enough. Even their organization, the Women's Liberation Association, was little known, except among socialist women's organizations abroad. American soldiers recognized its existence in battles such as Tet, and they endeavored to determine its leadership in any village they conquered. Being known was not what the Women's Liberation Association wanted. Anonymity was essential if the group or its members were to avoid reprisals and even capture, torture, or death.

Young women were excellent warriors because they were not tied to their families and could be trained to use weapons. (Vietnam News Service, Pike Collection)

Pictures taken by the Vietnam News Service made excellent propaganda for use in the Third World. These young people wore the floppy hats of the forces of the National Liberation Front and the traditional black pajamas. Scarves were common in the Mekong Delta. (Vietnam News Service, Pike Collection)

Women fought next to men in the fierce combat in the jungles and marshes of the Mekong Delta. (Vietnam News Service, Pike Collection)

These young women were determined fighters who were prepared to die to defend the fatherland. (Vietnam News Service, Pike Collection)

Women made excellent porters and could carry very heavy loads. (Courtesy of Vietnam Women's Union)

The best-known leader of the women's movement in the South was Nguyen Thi Dinh. (Courtesy of Vietnam Women's Union)

Nguyen Thi Dinh, who held a high position in the People's Liberation Armed Forces, instructed her young charges in the techniques of warfare. She was one of the founders of the National Liberation Front. (Courtesy of Vietnam Women's Union)

The women inspired by Nguyen Thi Dinh to fight loved their country and venerated Ho Chi Minh, who in this picture occupies a prominent place on the shelf to the ancestors. In his persona as Uncle Ho, father's elder brother, he was, literally, family. (Courtesy of Mel Halbach)

Women were taught how to handle a rifle using wooden guns. Real weapons were scarce; bullets, even scarcer. These soldiers are garbed in the typical dress of the Mekong Delta. (Vietnam News Service, Pike Collection)

Colonel Ho Thi Bi prided herself on her close association with Ho Chi Minh. In this picture, Bi is seated at the right hand of Uncle Ho. (Photo of a lithograph by Sandra C. Taylor, courtesy Ho Thi Bi)

Madame Nguyen Thi Binh, who became
the foreign minister of the National
Liberation Front. As a young woman,
she dressed in the simple attire of the
peasants. (Courtesy of Vietnam
Women's Union)

Madame Nguyen Thi Binh's most significant achievement was representing
(with Le Duc Tho) her country at the Paris peace talks. She is seated at the
head of the table, on the left, and is wearing a white blouse. (Courtesy of
Women's Museum, Hanoi)

Northern women learned how to fire weapons using telescopic sights and mortars. (Courtesy of Women's Museum, Hanoi, and Mel Halbach)

Duong Quynh Hoa, a physician in Ho Chi Minh City, was a founder of the National Liberation Front. (Courtesy of Mel Halbach)

Vo Thi Thang, the "smiling woman" who would not break despite repeated beatings, was arrested during a sapper attack in Saigon and sent to Con Dao. (Courtesy of Vietnam Women's Union)

The top of the tiger cages, from where lime was poured onto the prisoners below. (Courtesy of Mel Halbach)

Facing page: Quoc Nhut demonstrates the shackles in the tiger cages. (Courtesy of Mel Halbach)

Quoc Nhut in the tiger cage she occupied as a prisoner in Con Dao. (Courtesy of Mel Halbach)

Thieu Thi Tam and the guide at the Con Dao cemetery, near Vo Thi Sau's grave. (Photo by Sandra C. Taylor)

Liberation Radio broadcast from Hanoi to the South. Its frequent messages of encouragement included emulation tales and greetings from Nguyen Thi Dinh and Madame Nguyen Thi Binh. (Vietnam News Service, Pike Collection)

In the North, women and men wore French-style pith helmets to protect them from shrapnel and fire. These women are guarding the coastline. (Vietnam News Service, Pike Collection)

Defending Hanoi and cities of the North required special sites on weapons to detect high-flying American bombers. (Courtesy of Women's Museum, Hanoi)

Nguyen Thi Kim Lai leading captured American pilot Captain William Robinson to prison during the bombing of Hanoi. (Courtesy of Women's Museum, Hanoi)

This young woman wearing a pith helmet loads her weapon. She is probably a member of the Home Guard of the North. (Vietnam News Service, Pike Collection)

4

• • • • • • • • • • • • • • • •

THE LONG-HAIRED WARRIORS

What were these long-haired warriors like? From Communist literature comes a picture of unvarnished heroism, of women organizing armed uprisings and fighting with their sisters to win independence and liberty. One bit of propagandistic rhetoric indicates the role that the Party intended they should play: "Should we sit idly with our hands in our laps and look at the stars in the dark night and weep? No! That won't get us anywhere. We must rise up, and turn these sparkling dots into a sea of flames to light up the sky and burn out all the misery of our life of slavery."[1]

This exhortation typified the spirit the Party wished to instill, of women so inspired and dedicated that they not only would lead and follow others during the uprisings in the Mekong Delta, but would become the long-haired army that operated throughout the war.

At the beginning of the American conflict, women were ordered to follow the "three-pronged attack": spreading propaganda and recruiting, performing support services to the NLF, and harassing the ARVN and police. In addition, the women were to help transform their home areas into so-called fighting villages or combat townships, surrounded by bamboo spikes, with traps in which hidden sharpened stakes disabled the unwary enemy. These villages had fortifications such as berms, thick bamboo hedges, and tangled combat fences of barbed wire. Bunkers were dug to protect old people and children, additional underground spaces were excavated to hide guerrillas, and a "labyrinth of paths strewn with mines and spike-traps" ran among the peasants' huts.[2] From these combat townships, the women could work at destroying the "strategic hamlets" so prized by the Diem regime—villages in which peasants were herded together and forced to abandon their homes, ancestral graves, lands, crops, and animals, so that the enemy deemed Viet Cong by the Americans would be deprived of what Mao Zedong had termed the sea in which the Communist fish could swim. The American goal was to eliminate the friendly territory in which the revolutionaries could hide. Women were especially prized in these activities because they worked among their relatives and fellow villagers, and they could do these tasks at night while caring for their family.

The long-haired warriors, women who actually used weapons in combat, were the more obvious female combatants in the American war. The army that Nguyen Thi Dinh and her colleagues recruited was said by a Communist source to be 2 million strong by early 1967, armed with weapons that it had seized from the enemy.[3] This may have been a wildly inflated figure, but it indicated the goal, if not the actuality. Pictures of these young women are most dramatic: determined, bearing arms and dressed for battle in the black pajamas of the Vietnamese peasantry, often with the trademark black-and-white checkered neck scarf of the Mekong Delta around their necks. Photographers for the Front made sure that such pictures were given worldwide publicity.[4] Tribal women of the highlands, armed with crossbows, also made good subjects for skilled photographers. In addition to being models for photos, the long-haired army women were the subjects of drawings and paintings in the National Liberation Front publication, *South Vietnam in Struggle*. That the women could, on occasion, shoot well enough to bring down enemy aircraft, when such planes flew low enough to be vulnerable, was dramatic for photographers and evidence of the success of their training.[5] Although female guerrillas and militia whom the Americans and their allies might encounter as they conducted search-and-destroy operations in the countryside were usually supporters of the NLF, it was initially difficult for Westerners to realize that these women, who often were caring for small infants, could be killers.

If the Americans or South Vietnamese caught women who were young and armed, they assumed correctly that they were combatants. Liaison agents, scouts, spies, and "face-to-face" demonstrators could merge back into the general population once their tasks were done, and they were generally unarmed. Peasants carrying messages could always jump into the nearest rice paddy and resume farming when accosted; the local people, either supportive of the Front or, at best, afraid of its retaliation, would not betray them. Those who did so were often their own comrades, tortured until they revealed names. However, most members of the NLF did not know the real names of anyone. Stories of the guerrillas demonstrated the ingenuity of resistance among a people who were outgunned, but determined to fight until death. Their willingness to do battle, suffer torture and imprisonment, and even die attested to Communism's hold on them. It also showed their determination to gain independence, as well as the persistence of Nguyen Thi Dinh's saying, that there was "no other road to take."

Ideological motivation, stemming from the promises of Ho Chi Minh, was fostered by Liberation Radio broadcasts beamed from Hanoi. Women learned of press releases sent to friendly East European countries and the Third World; they heard documents meant for emulation campaigns stressing acts of heroism to be copied, and letters from well-known luminaries like Nguyen Thi Dinh and Madame Nguyen Thi Binh, the foreign minister of the Provisional Government of the NLF (a shadow government formed by Hanoi to prevent the guerrillas of the South from becoming too independent). Intellectuals were drawn in by the efforts of Duong Quynh Hoa, who was a Party member, and others in the NLF leadership who were not.[6]

Women of the Women's Liberation Association could act in extremely violent ways in the cities as well as the countryside. Vo Thi Thang was a sapper who operated in the Saigon area during the 1960s. She was captured and subjected to the standard tortures administered by the American-trained ARVN, which included beatings, use of electric probes and shocks, psychological torture, and other physical abuse, but she refused to give the names of her colleagues. She even had a smile on her face, which, according to Communist legend, remained despite her tortures. She was sentenced to twenty years of imprisonment on Con Dao, a punishment terminated only when the war ended in 1975. She told her tormentors that she smiled because she knew her side would win and they would lose, and she was right. After the war, she remained important in the Vietnam Women's Union and in 1998 was in charge of the Vietnam Tourist Bureau in Ho Chi Minh City.[7] City women, because they were more likely to be educated and ideologically committed, could be even more effective than village women; sometimes they were even harder to identify, since they could conceal their beliefs and actions among those of the general populace.

Some women, both urban and rural, came from families that had Communist roots dating from the 1930s or earlier, and they were part of a hard core of true believers. If others questioned Party ideology because of its wartime cruelties—the assassinations, murders, and extortions of taxes, food, and clothing to support the Front—the actions of the enemy persuaded them to remain loyal or at least neutral. The true believers questioned nothing.

As the war increased in violence, revenge for past brutality encouraged more people to take part. Dang Thi So, who lived on the outskirts of Chu Lai military base in the village of Dien Nam, Quang Ngai Province, the scene of continual and heavy fighting between the Americans and the NLF, phrased it clearly and succinctly: "I know our country was invaded by the aggressor, so I encouraged my sons to join the revolutionary Front." She described how her land had been bombed and destroyed, and then told how her sons had been killed. She herself participated in guerrilla warfare through the village Women's Liberation Association and was arrested and tortured many times. When she was incarcerated, she had to abandon her two smaller children, who were cared for by neighbors. By the end of the war, her health was broken and her husband and two sons were dead.[8] Hatred of the foreign invaders who killed her sons continued throughout her life. Yet sending more sons to fight and die, even after the first was killed, was a necessary sacrifice, not only for her but for other women. Whatever the revolution demanded, they would give.

Phan Thi Tao lived in the village of Hoa Hai, Quang-Nam Da-Nang Province. Her village was the site where, in 1965, the first American ground forces landed in Vietnam. The location, not far from the South China Sea, was sandwiched between the sandy beaches and the nearby jungle-covered mountains. To Tao, the American invasion was just like that of the French nearly a century earlier. Phan Thi Tao claimed that she had been part of an eleven-girl platoon that had, during the Tet offensive of 1968, "heroically pushed back a U.S. battalion counter-attack and killed 120 GIs." Since occasional references were made in later speeches about the heroism of the eleven-girl platoon, clearly something did happen, but it is very unlikely that such numbers could have been involved. A platoon perhaps, a company maybe, but certainly not a battalion.[9]

But the primary mission of Tao's unit was to provide service in a support division that carried enormous quantities of rice to the jungle, returning with wounded guerrillas who were taken to a nearby aid station. Her division was composed entirely of young women, most of whom were between the ages of fifteen and seventeen; she joined when she was nineteen. As the young women worked, they gradually became strong enough to carry massive loads; ultimately, they could haul burdens heavier than their body weight. Their routes went down the Ho Chi Minh Trail, into the forests, across streams and up steep banks, finally returning to villages along the coast. The girls suffered from malaria contracted in the jungle and grieved when they learned that family members had died in the fighting, but they did not contemplate quitting. Tao herself fought initially out of hatred for those who had killed her family, and she knew nothing of Communist ideology. But by the late 1960s, she was a committed ideologue who "believed in the future victory of the Communist Party and wanted revenge."[10] Many Vietnamese, despite the attraction of Communist ideology and idealism, fought for vengeance, a goal common to both sides.[11]

The women from Hoa Hai and surrounding villages had reason to fight, and they told their stories still grieving for their losses yet full of pride in the outcome of the war and optimistic about their country's future. The interviews conducted by the Rand Corporation present a different picture, perhaps more realistic because of the time the interviewers spent with their subjects, but no doubt influenced by the *chieu hoi*'s desire to demonstrate their innocence to their captors. One naive (or clever) interviewee was an aspiring singer who said she had joined the Front because it seemed fun— she could be an entertainer. Another young women was recruited because her mother beat her, and she wanted to get away from home. Others claimed that they had been forced to join, that they were afraid of the NLF, that they knew nothing and only did the cooking. Although some had been captured, others had chosen to change sides and might well change sides again.[12]

Although the *dong khoi* uprisings in Ben Tre occurred in early January 1960, women are not mentioned as armed warriors until the establishment of the National Liberation Front and the Women's Liberation Association in 1961 and the People's Revolutionary Party (PRP) in January 1962. A few exceptional women, such as Nguyen Thi Dinh and Ho Thi Bi, were armed and fighting in early 1960, as were others whose military careers dated from French times, but the NLF did not have sufficient weapons to arm and train many women when the American conflict began. The literature on women's roles stressed the "three-pronged attack" rather than combat. Women were expected to perform traditional roles, working in the rear, supporting the warriors but not being part of them, and carrying out political activism. After battles, they nursed as well as cooked and cared for the forces of the Front.

Before the founding of the PRP, activities were coordinated by the Southern Branch of the North Vietnamese Workers' Party (Lao Dong), which was the successor to the Indochinese Communist Party. Soon after the establishment of the Women's Association and the NLF, Communist women were organized into two types. "Legal" guerrilla units operated in "liberated areas," or territory controlled by the NLF. "Illegal" guerrilla units operated in enemy territory, where the members had to obtain GVN identification documents by deception, permitting them to move about, or in areas where ultimate control was in dispute.[13] With the organization of guerrilla units in liberated areas, young women who showed an aptitude for and an interest in combat were trained and armed, especially in regions of intense fighting. They were most often in their late teens and early twenties, since the Party found that young people, aged sixteen (the age when they could join the Women's Liberation Association) and older, were more enthusiastic and less fearful of death than those in their mid-twenties and older. Young women were also more likely to be single, and hence more mobile. By 1969, six women from the Thua Thien-Hue District had been awarded the distinction of Hero of the People's Liberation Armed Forces.[14]

The elderly, even if they did support the Front, were often horrified that the girls would leave home to work among men, acting "without care or caution," not like traditional young women.[15] Old women feared the breakdown in morals among the young, who would be living with others of the opposite sex, while their own parents were more often simply afraid they would be killed.[16] Yet their parents had to encourage them to participate or risk being labeled as reactionaries.

The sobriquet "long-haired army" (or warriors) appeared in many documents that the NLF wrote for internal use, especially in emulation tales, but it also was the subject of an article written in 1966 for the journal *Viet Nam Studies*, which had an international audience.[17] "Fierce Fight by the Long-Haired Army," an article written in 1969, is typical of the popularization of the phrase. It related the story of a woman called Sister Bay, who led a group of more than 200 women insurgents in the My Long District of Ben Tre Province. Sister Bay landed her boat, led her squad to the riverbank, and "waved a big NFL [sic] flag and shouted, 'Forward!'" She and her supporters overran the administrative headquarters of the village, and when she was cut down as she tried to plant a flag on the government building, her followers immediately rushed to replace her. They succeeded in fixing the flag in position.[18]

The origin of the term "long-haired warriors," or women with long hair, is obscure. In Mai Van Elliot's transcription of the memoir of Nguyen Thi Dinh, *No Other Road to Take*, Dinh stated that it was applied to the women who in 1960 carried out the "face-to-face" struggles with the enemy, marching en masse to the local Saigon government headquarters and demanding a stop to atrocities and compensation for deaths the troops had caused.[19] The term outlasted the uprising. One account is that Ho Chi Minh awarded this name to Nguyen Thi Dinh and the women of the Ben Tre uprising for their exceptional bravery; then it gradually spread (with his blessing) to include all the women in the NLF. Other sources attribute it to Ngo Dinh Diem, who would not have used it as a term of praise, but to condemn these unfeminine women. Among historians, there is further dispute. William Duiker states that the women porters of Dien Bien Phu were referred to as the long-haired army, while Douglas Pike, a specialist on the Viet Cong, says that only southern women bore the appellation. The official guide at the Vietnam Women's Union in Hanoi, Dinh Thi Van, who had fought in both North and South during the war, insisted that the phrase applied only to southern women.[20] A history of the women of Vietnam applies it to the South,[21] as does the brochure of the Women's Museum in Ho Chi Minh City.

Training documents written during the war reminded members of the Women's Liberation Association of the phrase, as they reaffirmed the Communists' policy toward women. In a captured document from the Saigon Gia-Dinh area dated 1966, the NLF told its followers that "millions of women have participated in the direct struggle . . . they have contributed to the revolution by joining the army." The heroic example of Nguyen Thi Dinh was always cited, and in this document she and two other women were singled out as especially meritorious. Twenty-three other women in the South who had killed Americans were also cited for special merit. The writer exhorted them: "Women must lead in the struggle to send the Americans home."[22]

Other women were also listed among those to emulate, and the Front even set up a "schedule of awards for 'American-killing units' and individual 'American-killers.'"[23] Even though these particular heroines were not identified as members of the long-haired army, their exploits justified the appellation. By the mid-1960s, Dinh was leading troops in Ben Tre District. Vo Thi Mo was fighting at Cu Chi, the anonymous woman of An Giang was shooting American and ARVN troops, women from Hue had joined the PAVN and had organized into guerrilla units, and individual women were killing the enemy, often not even using rifles, according to NLF documents. Some of these fighters were very creative, making mines from empty fuel barrels, stuffing them with iron scraps, and letting the weight of Americans passing overhead explode them. A captured propaganda leaflet told emulation stories of numerous brave and heroic women. One tribal woman in the People's Liberation Armed Forces had made "1,620 trips [down the Ho Chi Minh Trail] averaging fifty-five kilos [120 pounds] per trip." Since she was not an ethnic Vietnamese from the Delta, she was not technically a long-haired warrior, but she certainly had served the cause of the revolution. Another minority woman, Kan Lich of the Pako tribe of Thua Thien Province, was described as having accomplished "feats as a guerilla leader [that] still strike fear among Saigon soldiers." She crawled into an enemy post, awakened the inhabitants, and then shot many of them. When asked why she woke her victims, she replied, "I wanted to know exactly how many of them were killed."[24] For this accomplishment, she was named a Heroine of the South Vietnam People's Liberation Armed Forces. She appeared to have worked alone on this mission, but judging from her importance in 1969, presumably she had fought with the People's Liberation Armed Forces for some time. She was a Vietnam Army officer in 1997.

These women's ancestors had been members of the Viet Minh, combatants whether or not they were called long-haired warriors.[25] Their stories, even if apocryphal, inculcated determination and courage into those who read and studied them. In some cases, the women I interviewed were from districts where rebellion had existed since 1945. Women from the Women's Union in the village of Thuy Phuong, Thua Thien-Hue Province, met to tell me their stories. They explained proudly that their village was the "first place where women stood up to fight with American troops."[26] Its location was critical, being four miles from Hue, the old imperial capital of Vietnam, on a narrow strip of land between the sea and the mountains. Guerrillas had been based there since French times. The Americans made the spot into a "no-man's land" by the use of defoliants in an attempt to destroy it as a revolutionary base. But before that, it had been the location of the "Street Without Joy," the site described by French author Bernard Fall, where French Highway 1 was repeatedly cut by the Viet Minh.[27] The French soldiers sent there knew of its reputation and feared, rightly, for their lives. After 1975, the village was awarded "heroic village" status, and one of its citizens, Nguyen Thi Lai, a retired colonel, received the title of Hero of the Vietnamese National Army. The women of this village remembered the war vividly, in part because the "white zone," or no-man's land, lay all around them—bleak, infertile, and desolate, twenty-five years after the war's end. One woman, Tran Thu Ha, explained that since the village population had consisted of many women (the men had joined the People's Liberation Armed Forces), they were ordered to form guerrilla units there. She joined, although an American camp was based in the village. Ha continued to proselytize, recruiting more soldiers for the Tet Offensive of 1968. After the battle, the Americans counterattacked and attempted to destroy all resistance in the village. But they were unsuccessful. Ha and the others hid in underground shelters during the day, and at night returned aboveground to recruit soldiers and obtain food for the Front. In 1995, Ha was just forty-seven years old, although her experiences made her look far older. She said that she had been fortunate to survive imprisonment and torture, and, after liberation, to marry and have four sons.[28]

One seventy-six-year-old woman, Nguyen Thi Luong, was very frail, with a crippled body, teeth stained black with betel juice, and almost no hair, but she told of her battle experience with gusto. She had joined the Viet Minh and fought in a battle with the French in 1944; their camp, like the Americans' twenty years later, was located in this strategic area. She joined the women's movement in 1946, and was soon a member of a sapper unit, a demolition and assassination force that used grenades or hand weapons and was prepared to die in the act. She was also in the intelligence force in Hue and was, by then, a member of the Communist Party. In 1952, her husband was killed, leaving her with a son, her only child. During the American war, she was no longer a soldier, but was told by the Party to be a messenger and then to lead a division to transfer supplies to the NLF. Her wartime service never really ended, for she was arrested in 1962 and held for three years, tormented with electric shocks and then subjected to the water torture, by which soldiers poured soapy water into her mouth until no more could be forced and then jumped on her stomach, expelling the fluid out of every orifice. She said, "I considered them [my captors] like animals except that animals are not as cruel as this." Her son, who had joined the NLF and was part of a three-man sapper squad, died when his unit tried to attack an American military outpost in a nearby village.

As were so many others, Luong was released from prison and returned to Hue to work with the women's movement; she was commanded to transfer orders from the provincial Party Committee to the local. But she had to think of a disguise so that she would not be suspect if she was detained. Her way, that of a "white-haired woman," was to pretend to be mad. When she was stopped by enemy soldiers and told to eat dog feces to prove that she was crazy, she did so. She went about without any clothes except for a sash around her waist in which she hid the messages, and she slept, unclothed, in the dirt. Soon she could freely enter the American military base, where she begged. There, she obtained information on troop movements from sympathetic South Vietnamese soldiers. She transmitted this intelligence to the NLF, which used it in planning its attacks. In carrying out this ploy for five years, she was occasionally arrested, but her disguise served her well. Even the doctor who examined her concluded that she was crazy. When she told the enemy that she was a Communist, they did not believe her. Once when she was accosted and asked whom she preferred, the Saigon forces or the National Liberation Front, she said she liked them both because they were all sons and daughters of the dragon (the mythical figure that gave birth to Vietnam). Again, such an answer was considered proof of madness. The only thing that almost broke her spirit was the news of her son's death, which she received two years after he died. But she swore that she would get revenge, so she repressed her tears and worked twice as hard, doing his work as well as her own.[29]

Luong told me of other women who had fought in French times and continued to resist foreign domination. One seventy-five-year-old woman, Le Thi Vit, had participated in the August Revolution of 1945, becoming a Party member in 1949. She worked with the Viet Minh, and when the American war began, she continued the struggle. Even when her village was forced into a strategic hamlet, she continued her work by recruiting young people. Her special task became the hiding of NLF guerrillas, and she was not deterred even when soldiers caught and beat her. She bragged that she had hidden thirteen Communist soldiers in her underground shelter and a company of ARVN had commandeered her rather spacious house. The Saigon soldiers, there for three days, never discovered the presence of the enemy beneath them. Vit smuggled food to the NLF forces and emptied chamber pots for them, while she hosted their enemy in her home. The ARVN soldiers knew that there were Communists in the village, but they never found them. Finally, they left her family alone.[30] She, like Luong, considered resistance a duty in line with the precept: "When the enemy comes, even women have to fight."

The increasing number of women involved in combat, as fighters or support personnel, may have contributed to the debate that occurred in late 1967 in the American military, particularly between General William Westmoreland and his staff, about the so-called cross-over point. Westmoreland believed that the People's Army of Vietnam and the full-time fighting forces of the NLF would eventually be killed at such a rate that they would not be able to be replaced. At that point, the Communists would be eliminated and Ho Chi Minh would have to concede. However, Westmoreland refused to accept the argument advanced by intelligence operatives of the Central Intelligence Agency, notably Samuel Adams, that local self-defense forces, who were often unarmed (in terms of conventional weapons) and who fought only part-time, were an integral part of the enemy forces. If Westmoreland's figures about the number of enemy troops were accepted as correct, then the strategy of attrition, wearing down the enemy by killing them off, was working. Since the American military was largely unaware of the number of women involved in the fighting and the often unorthodox manner in which they fought, the strategic planners had miscalculated. While not all women carried weapons and few fought full-time, they were mobilized through the Women's Association and were a fundamental part of the Front. Certainly by the end of 1967, countless women were involved in the resistance, which would become apparent during the Tet Offensive.[31]

Women also were not as suspect as men when the United States military began the program known as Operation Phoenix, the elimination of what they called the Viet Cong Infrastructure, in an attempt to destroy the NLF. Again, since the women were rarely top-level cadre, they were less noticeable than men. However, they were still purposely killed, as the author of the program, William Colby, a former CIA station chief in Saigon, noted. While maintaining, as he did throughout his life, that random killing was much less frequent than critics of Phoenix charged, Colby related one incident that he had witnessed in which a district chief had "jumped out of his jeep and shot [a female Communist leader]." The man was immediately dismissed by his superior, but the province adviser told Colby that this woman "had been directly responsible for the deaths of several members of the Chief's family."[32] That, of course, made killing her acceptable—another example of "rough justice," much like the incident during Tet when Saigon police chief Nguyen Ngoc Loan summarily executed a guerrilla. This bloody scene, carried out in the street, gave the photographer fame in the annals of photojournalism.[33] Killing the woman was just another act of war.

It was uncommon, but certainly not unknown, for women to join the People's Liberation Armed Forces. In May 1968, correspondent Beverly Deepe of the *Christian Science Monitor* wrote that an American air-mobile operation had killed women guerrillas and captured others on the battlefields; one woman, she noted, had been toting a sixty-five-pound minigun taken from an American helicopter. She also stated that in Dalat, an "all-women Viet Cong company several months ago charged and disabled a platoon-sized Vietnamese government outpost and later killed three American advisers and the brother of a Vietnamese general who led in reinforcements."[34] In preparations for the Tet Offensive, more women than ever before had been "mobilized to serve on the front line"; they were also used to recruit youths for the Assault Youth Groups and to obtain civilian laborers. The NLF was said to have activated "a platoon of female civilian laborers working on a full-time basis." Women were reminded that they had a quota to meet: 50 percent of the guerrilla strength in the lowlands and 12 percent in the highlands should be female. Women, after all, could kill the enemy with "ordinary, crude, and home-made weapons."[35]

Most women who fought did so in one of three ways: in village militia, which often were unarmed; as part of assassination squads or sapper units; or as guerrillas, fighting as part of a female contingent of paramilitary units in hamlets or villages. At first, female guerrillas had rudimentary weapons and could obtain rifles, pistols, and machine guns only if they captured them from the enemy. Colonel Ho Thi Bi of Ho Chi Minh City exemplified this mode, and her story indicated that the practice went back to the French war. The women's primary weapons were those of the most primitive sort: devices made to trap soldiers in ambushes, *punji* stakes to place in the sides and bottoms of pits, and explosive devices made from unexploded ordnance. The soldiers of the Front were divided into main forces, local forces, and guerrillas, and the third category was most suited to women because they could "be a soldier when the enemy comes and a civilian when he leaves." Women, as a captured document from 1966 noted, "have much capacity for this [type of] war."[36]

The statement's author, though, condemned all the local forces for the weakness of their will to fight. Recruitment was key, for both men and women, and the NLF was urged to train female guards and snipers, as well as farmers. The writer noted that "white-haired units," the elderly, were also useful.[37] Killing women, children, and the elderly, even if they were most likely the enemy, at first caused American troops difficulties, as one veteran, Richard Stevens, related in his book on the Ho Chi Minh Trail.[38] But they soon got used to it.

By 1967, the long-haired warriors were not only more numerous but more effective. Nguyen Thi Dinh, in a talk on Liberation Radio, praised this "intrepid corps" who had carried out "face-to-face" and local autonomous struggles, and had stopped the advance of enemy tanks by lying down in front of the oncoming vehicles. However, that was not true everywhere. An "absolute secret" resolution captured in May 1967 in Thua Thien Province complained that although there had been numerous victories in that area, there were still too few guerrillas. Guerrillas made up less than 1 percent of the population. Women, the anonymous author warned, were "still disregarded and are not recruited for the guerrilla force." The solution was to enlist more from the working classes, "families who have animosity [toward] the enemy. . . . [W]e should try to bring the ratio of militia women to 50–60% of the total militia force." Later in the document, the Party cadre called for the development of more guerrilla and self-defense forces, especially the young, women, old men, and old women: there should be 50 percent females among the guerrillas, and 5 percent "white-haired" units.[39]

The discrepancy—stories of heroism in the midst of calls for additional efforts at recruitment—can be attributed to two things. One was the nature of the war: as combat intensified, people dropped out through fear, or they were wounded or killed. The GVN's policy was to separate the people from the Front, and as they did so, they did "dry up the sea." The program of pacification, "winning hearts and minds," as President John Kennedy called it, did have some successes. The second reason for the nature of such exhortations drew on Communist techniques for propagandizing. Self-criticism was a standard means of urging people to do more, to condemn themselves for not having achieved enough. Many reports captured from the enemy were replete with self-condemnations by the authors for having failed to meet a quota. The Americans were not the only ones to inflate the "body count"; the NLF also wanted its numbers to look good in Hanoi's eyes, so it tended to enlarge them. The Front did, however, categorize its recruits according to the degree of their commitment and work on strengthening the determination of those who were weak. But people are human, and in the face of the real likelihood of death, both men and women took advantage of the South's *chieu hoi* program and defected to the other side—at least for a while.

The Tet Offensive, celebrating the lunar new year of Mau Than, the monkey, 1968 on the Western calendar, brought women out in force throughout the South. Captured documents from as far back as November 1967 indicated that a major offensive was in the offing. The problem for Westmoreland's staff was determining where it would take place. Since major fighting had begun at Khe Sanh, there was much speculation that the new battle was designed to be another Dien Bien Phu. However, such was not the case; beginning on January 31, 1968, NLF sapper squads attacked most of the major cities of the South, anticipating that the population would rise up and there would be a general offensive. Women guerrillas as well as men were active in the widespread attacks, but only in Hue did the guerrillas succeed in holding a city for any length of time. Hue was controlled by the guerrillas for twenty-five days, and it was regained only in fierce fighting that led to severe loss of life on both sides. There were actually three waves to the Tet Offensive, the last one in May. The total NLF casualties were horrendous, in some cases amounting to almost total destruction. But Hanoi persisted in calling Tet a success, and as a psychological victory, it was.[40]

In assessing the offensive in 1970, Communist literature praised women's achievements. An anonymous writer from Binh Dinh Province described the "female armed combat units which fought in enemy areas." Four women were singled out, along with "the May [third wave] female artillery units of the female nationalities in Lam Dong province."[41] Many other women fought in Saigon. Hoang Thi Khanh smuggled arms into the city and recruited people to support the revolution. Khanh had been transferred from the countryside to Saigon in 1967 as part of a sapper force, serving as a liaison with the countryside as well as smuggling arms. Before the outbreak of the Tet Offensive, she brought guerrillas into the city and helped coordinate them once the fighting started. When the offensive inside the city failed, she reorganized the troops who were still alive in preparation for a counterattack. She herself led troops, 80 percent of whom were women, since it was easier to smuggle women into the city than men. During the fighting, her troops managed to kill some of the South Vietnamese enemy, whom she described as "very dangerous people who knew who the revolutionaries were." She was finally caught in November 1969 when she was proselytizing in Saigon and was put on a truck with other Communists to be taken to prison. Although she was carrying documents, she tried to persuade her captors that she was illiterate and thus could not read them. It was to no avail; she was sentenced to prison and was moved from Tan Hiep prison to the island of Con Dao. She said that she had been convinced to support the revolution because she, a poverty-stricken peasant, sided with the poor and oppressed. Khanh, in 1995 the head of the Federation of Labor Unions in Ho Chi Minh City, was a powerful woman whose beliefs have remained unchanged.[42]

Other women did similar jobs during Tet. The sisters Thieu Thi Tam and Thieu Thi Tao, teenagers who supported the Front, began their revolutionary activities early. Tam had joined the resistance when she was ten; in 1964, she had attempted to burn herself alive by emulating the actions of the monk who immolated himself at an intersection in Saigon, but the monks pulled her back. The sisters then tried to set off a bomb at the Saigon police headquarters, which was also the location of the CIA. They were captured and interrogated; their captors called them the Hai Ba Trung, the famous Trung sisters reincarnated. When torturing them was to no avail, they, with many other women and girls, were imprisoned. They were sent to Con Dao. At fifteen, Tam was the youngest prisoner on the island; the imprisonment of one so young sparked protests around the world.[43]

This prison was especially hard on women, whether they were in the infamous "tiger cages," which held from two to five prisoners, shackled to the concrete floor, or in the open cells to which Tam and Tao were sent. The top of the tiger-cage cell blocs was open, covered with only iron rods, so the jailers could drop lime on the prisoners when they had been beaten or had disobeyed orders. One woman, Nguyen Thi Thu An, who had been arrested for smuggling arms into Saigon, returned to Con Dao with her daughter in 1994. She had been in the tiger cages, and even the sight of the one she had inhabited brought tears to her eyes. She related how poorly they were fed, how they had to supplement their meager rations of rice gruel with dead birds or geckos they caught, and how they gave that bit of protein to whomever in the cell was closest to death. The cell was packed with prisoners when the weather was hot, and left with only two when it was cold. The women had no sanitary facilities during their menstrual periods and had to tear the sleeves off their shirts to use as protection. They had no privacy and almost no opportunity to bathe. But the experience—if they survived— hardened them, as it did the men. Thu An remained a Party member in 1995. The island at that time contained a memorial to the prisoners in the small cemetery outside the prison walls as well as a statue to Vo Thi Sau, the young girl killed by the French in 1952. The prison itself was liberated in 1975.[44]

Women were commended for their military actions during the Tet Offensive in publications in the North. One pamphlet praised the workers who had struggled during the uprising and noted with satisfaction that the struggle had now made the cities as well as the countryside into battlefields.

One episode during Tet attracted considerable attention. The gist of the account had to do with the actions of eleven young women who had variously "killed hundreds of American aggressors."[45] An article by Nguyen Dinh Chi, the vice president of the Vietnam Alliance of National, Democratic, and Peace Forces, also reported that "eleven girls had repulsed an American battalion in Hue." She described how "one Hue mother, together with the liberation troops, captured one American colonel of the intelligence service,"[46] and many other armed women had also engaged the enemy.[47] The similarity of this story to the one related to me by Phan The Tao, also one of heroism by eleven girls in Hue during the Tet Offensive, indicates that something happened. But by 1995 it had taken on the characteristics of an urban legend.

The women who had fought in Saigon and other locations during Tet were widely praised. A radio broadcast to Eastern Europe stated that they "drove back a whole battalion after nearly a hundred fights inside and outside the city [Saigon]."[48] A self-defense force composed of teenagers was commended for having attacked Tan Son Nhut airfield and two other locations in Saigon. The long-haired fighters in Ben Tre Province had forced their adversaries out of thirty-six posts, and a report noted the "valiant efforts of an unarmed Khmer girl." It also mentioned that 100,000 women followers of the Cao Dai church had struggled against "savage massacres within its holy see at Tay Ninh."[49] But other documents pointed out that unarmed women and children had fled the bombing everywhere and often had been its victims.

The area of Cu Chi, in a district about fifteen miles west of Saigon, earned the appellation "iron land" for its resistance to conquest by government forces. During Tet, it was the scene of major battles, and many of the arms and combatants for the offensive were moved from there to Saigon. Cu Chi's inhabitants, who were driven into the arms of the NLF by their resistance to the high-tech warfare to which they were subjected, found their only safety in tunnels. The vast tunnel complex, 200 miles long, not only provided hiding places for Viet Cong, but contained underground hospitals, spaces where entertainment troops could propagandize through song, and staging areas for military operations. The tunnels were such effective hiding places that their very existence was not suspected until 1968.[50]

Women helped to construct these underground chambers, digging them slowly and painstakingly by hand or with a tool as small as a teaspoon. They carefully disposed of the earth, spreading it over the surface of the land or dumping it into a nearby river, so that the American and ARVN forces would not detect it. They camouflaged the entrances to the tunnels so that they could not be seen from above. They nursed the injured, buried the dead—in the tunnel walls if graves could not be dug aboveground—prepared food, and entertained people living inside. Like the men, they suffered from the claustrophobic conditions, the foul air, and the fear of bombs, injuries, and illness. Conditions inside the tunnels were especially hard on women. They were unable to bathe or to cleanse themselves, even during their menstrual periods. Sanitary conditions deteriorated even more when the fighting made it impossible to leave the subterranean chambers for long periods of time. Spending months underground had a deleterious effect on mental health as well.

Women fought against American and ARVN soldiers as part of male units, but Cu Chi also had an all-female fighting force, the C3 Company, which was formed in 1965. The unit was led by Tran Thi Dung, a teenager who died of an illness in 1973. All the women were skilled in firing small arms, throwing grenades, wiring and detonating mines, and assassination. Vo Thi Mo became a deputy leader of the women's platoon. She came from a family of eleven children, three of whom had been killed in the war. Her family had escaped the destruction of their home by entering the tunnels through a bunker outside it, and she determined, at the age of fifteen, to fight against the invaders who were destroying her land.[51]

The young women in Mo's squad were enthusiastic about their mission. Their first real battle was against two American tanks moving down a mined and booby-trapped road. The tanks were stopped by the mines; one was put out of commission, but the other was later repaired by the enemy. Although the action was a standoff rather than a victory, it was an amazing accomplishment for a few teenagers and a ten-year-old boy.[52]

Although they could handle weapons, the girls were discouraged from engaging in hand-to-hand combat with the Americans because of their youth and small stature. They were very effective in organizing a spy ring that penetrated the Twenty-fifth Infantry Division base next to Cu Chi. Vo Thi Mo was also skilled as an assassin and killed several Americans bathing in a bomb crater outside the base. She led a raid on a large ARVN military post nearby, surrounded by barbed wire. She crossed the wire with her comrades and took two prisoners, who were astonished and probably caught off guard by the sight of Mo minus her trousers, which had been snagged by the barbed wire.[53]

During the Tet Offensive, fighting at Cu Chi was heavy. Vo Thi Mo, by now an accomplished and successful combatant, was wounded in the battles. While in the hospital, she received a personal telegram from Madame Nguyen Thi Binh, then a member of the Central Committee of the NLF and soon to gain world fame as its chief diplomat during the Paris peace talks, announcing the award of Victory Medal Class Three (in the highest category of medal) to the entire female platoon. After Mo returned to combat, she reflected to British interviewers that she was even more obsessed by her hatred of Americans.[54]

The only peculiar incident in the successful military career of this young fighter occurred after her recovery. While she was on patrol with her squad, there were a series of battles with the Americans. Her comrades pulled back to rest, but Mo continued on, accompanied by the boy messenger. They observed three Americans sitting down, eating snacks, and sharing photographs. The soldiers became very emotional and even started crying. Mo was stunned by this; perhaps they, too, were human. Although she would have received the Victory Medal Class One if she had killed them, she could not bring herself to do it. She was the subject of a Party inquiry as a result, but was not punished. It is hard to say why not—perhaps she was too good a soldier, and her superiors hesitated to blemish her record. Why the Americans exposed themselves to such danger is equally puzzling; the journalists reporting her story thought that perhaps they were high on marijuana.[55]

Mo remained with the famous C3 Women's Company until the end of the war. By this time, she had married. She, her husband, and her parents moved to a village in Tay Ninh, since their house in Cu Chi had been destroyed. They began a new family life there.[56]

There were other all-women's guerrilla units in the South. The third All-South Women Mobilizing Cadres Conference met on February 5, 1970, to review the situation of southern women; after a week, they issued a communiqué over Liberation Radio. Among the many groups to be praised was "the female armed combat units which fought in enemy areas, represented by such female heroes as Nguyen Thi Lai, Mai Thi Mong, Nguyen Viet Hong, Vo The Anh, the 8 March female artillery units of the female nationalities [probably minority women] in Lam Dong province and so forth."[57] A newspaper article spoke of a company named in honor of Nguyen Thi Minh Khai in south-central Vietnam, the "803 women guerrilla unit of Lam Dong, the Phuoc Long platoon, and many women artillery units of Long An, Tay Ninh, Binh Long, My Tho, Ben Tre, Gia Dinh, Binh Duong, Rach Gia, Xuan Loc provinces and of the Binh Duc belt etc., which have scored outstanding military feats in destroying the enemy strength."[58] By 1970, women not only were organized, but had acquired weapons and knew how to use them. They remained a minority of the forces of the NLF, but they posed a problem for their enemy by their very existence. Guerrillas were always hard to identify, since the men did not wear uniforms or behave as traditional soldiers did, but women guerrillas were even more unusual and more difficult to identify.

The successes women had often were in individual actions or three-person cells. Nguyen Thi Lai, the decorated colonel of the Vietnamese National Army from the village of Thuy Phuong, threw a steel milk container at an American tank; the men inside thought that she was lobbing a grenade and, in their confusion, tipped over the tank on a bridge, "killing many Americans." The spokeswoman for the Vietnam Women's Union at Thuy Phuong related, "In the first battle in 1966, the woman Nguyen Viet Phong was the commander of a three-person squad and they attacked one American battalion and they [the soldiers] ran."[59] The accounting of such feats achieved the desired result of inspiring others to fight.

The Party doctrine of "emulating heroines" led to the honoring of specific women and units. Some women were awarded medals, and they were often publicized in the Party newspaper or proselytizing documents of a given region. If a woman was deemed worthy enough, she might have an entire story written about her, as in the case of Ut Tich.

Emulating heroines was a good way of bringing in recruits and stimulating those already in the Front to fight harder. International Women's Day, March 8, also marked the founding of the Women's Liberation Association, and it was an appropriate time to celebrate Vietnam's revolutionary heroines. Each year after 1961, they were acclaimed in speeches broadcast over the clandestine radio of the Front and in articles in the Hanoi newspaper *Nhan Dan*. On March 7, 1970, the South Vietnam Women's Liberation Association marked the occasion with an "accelerated emulation drive" honoring the achievements of southern women—from the embroidering of napkins with struggle mottos to the displaying and weaving of hair from the heads of women who opposed the regime while in jail. The napkins and woven hair were smuggled out of prisons, and they were, in 1995, on display in the women's museums in Hanoi and Ho Chi Minh City. One article about such keepsakes noted with great pride that there were other mementos, such as "the souveniers [*sic*] of seven cartridges from a female assault team that had annihilated four Americans."[60]

The association of the embroidered napkins with the spent cartridges is interesting. As Cynthia Enloe has remarked, "wartime embroidery [was] evidence that a woman who engaged in anti-colonial politics was a feminine woman all the while. . . . [F]emininity's compatibility with otherwise disruptive nationalist wartime mobilization" was, according to Enloe, a theme that ran throughout war efforts in Vietnam and elsewhere.[61] The women's museums give ample testimony to such creative and distinctively feminine endeavors as embroidery—juxtaposed with rifles, pictures of long-haired warriors, and photographs of the horrors of war.

The statement on women's achievements, clandestinely broadcast over Liberation Radio, found much to praise. Aside from publications on wartime exploits, the women's press, Phu Nu Giai Phong (Women's Liberation), founded in 1970, had published books on protecting the lives and health of women and children, an important postwar goal of the Women's Union. The attendees at the March 7 celebration were also impressive. They included representatives of the women working in various branches of the PLAF as well as delegations of mass organizations, women from the mountain tribes as well as the shock youth force (probably a sapper squad).[62]

Not all women were Party members or guerrillas fighting in the jungles, but they, like many men, believed in the ideals of independence from foreign intervention and freedom. Such women composed a "third force," in between the extremes of the Saigon regime and its American connection and the hard core of Communist Party resistance. Some of these women eventually became Party members, while others tried to mediate for peace. Generally urban intellectuals, they also advocated human rights, justice, and the rights of women. The movement included teachers, professors, journalists, physicians, engineers, architects, writers, and even Buddhist nuns. The third force existed from the beginnings of the resistance movement in Vietnam and stemmed from the ideas of Phan Boi Chau and Phan Chu Trinh, both of whom were strong patriots in the early decades of the twentieth century whose concepts of resistance and independence were not as radical as those of Ho Chi Minh. However, the leadership of the Party sought the support of the third force because of its prestige among the people.[63]

The third force movement was particularly appealing to the urban elite, since open Party membership among them during the French and the American-supported regimes in Saigon would have resulted in imprisonment and death. They considered themselves patriots first and foremost, as did Party members, but to the French and Americans their activities and the groups they founded and joined were little better than Communist front organizations. Many of the most well known women in the South were part of the third force. Duong Quynh Hoa was such a woman, although she combined Party membership with her patriotism.

Because the third force was not a single organization but a loose coalition, it included regional movements such as the Association to Protect Women's Dignity and Rights, founded in 1966 by a teacher of literature at Gia Long High School named Phan Thi Cua. Its membership consisted of many female writers and artists in Saigon. The Peace Protection Movement and the Vietnam Alliance of National, Democratic, and Peace Forces, of which Hoa was a member, was another Saigon-based component. Ngo Ba Thanh, professor of international law at the University of Saigon, who had obtained a Ph.D. from Columbia University, formed the Women's Right to Life Association in 1970. Its aim was to press the Thieu government to work for peace and an end to war. She was arrested in 1971 for having organized an "illegal organization" and protested the one-man presidential election of Thieu.[64]

Nguyen Phuc Dai, a prominent lawyer in Saigon, also worked with this group. In 1971, the Women's Right to Life Association signed an accord with the Women's International League for Peace and Freedom (WILPF), an important attempt to build bridges between pacifist women whose love of peace transcended national boundaries. By this time, the urgency to reach a peaceful settlement had brought some thirteen Vietnamese women's groups together, and even the signing of the Paris Peace Accords on January 23, 1973, which specified the withdrawal of American forces two months later, did not silence these advocates of peace. For them, the war lasted another two years.

Among the groups advocating peace and opposing the American aggressors and their Saigon supporters was the Vietnam Buddhist Nuns' Association. Its president, Huynh Lien, was a strong champion of nonviolence, as was the nun Ngoc Lien. They participated in demonstrations in Saigon and helped make the pagodas into sources of resistance to the regimes of Diem and Thieu. Two nuns, Tri Tuc and Nguyen Thi Kieu, immolated themselves in Can Tho in March 1967, and a Buddhist student, Nhat Chi Mai, also killed herself. Since Buddhism advocated peace and religious freedom, opposition to the long and bloody war was an important component of the Buddhist third force.[65]

The third force, which the Americans had once advocated as the best alternative to colonialism or Communism, could not exist by itself once the United States entered the war. The military tactics it used forced the Vietnamese to take sides. Since neutrality or pacifism was not a possibility, many city women identified more closely with the NLF, although they might have preferred to support an organization like the Women's Right to Life Association. To the Americans, all such groups were Communist fronts. There were only two choices—no third force.

5

• • • • • • • • • • • • • • • •

YOUTH AT WAR

The conflict that engulfed Vietnam from 1945 to 1975 was a "family affair," not only a war for independence from foreign control, but a struggle that frequently included all family members. One story in the Communist newspaper, *South Viet Nam in Struggle,* recounted how a man, "Loi," and his son and daughter destroyed a helicopter. They had been disturbed by helicopters flying over their fields at night, killing people and destroying their crops. The father and fifteen-year-old son determined to shoot down a helicopter and dug a gun emplacement. The young sister helped by sounding a warning with a bamboo tocsin. They fired at the enemy aircraft but failed to hit it, and the pilot laughed at their efforts. Angered, the father shot again as the helicopter lowered, and the craft, damaged, crashed. The villagers celebrated the feats of the father, son, and daughter. Soon, gun emplacements were to be found throughout the region.[1]

Although long-haired warriors like Tran Thi Ly and the comrades of Nguyen Thi Dinh were young women in their late teens and early twenties, children and women of all age groups participated in the struggle. Photographs depicting women armed to fight show their youth, their determination, and their apparent ease in handling weapons. Young women from peasant villages were easily convinced to fight back by the propaganda of the revolution, the injustices of the Saigon government, and the carnage of war. Their siblings and parents were guerrillas, and sometimes their sweethearts were as well. Often they came from "liberated" villages under the control of the Front. The husbands of women often fought for the NLF, coming and going from the village under cover of darkness, and a couple's children could help the cause. The grandparents often had been fighters in the war with the French, and the American war was simply a continuation of the long struggle for independence.

One story that captured the imagination of the world came with the execution of a young man, Nguyen Van Troi. Troi had attempted to assassinate Secretary of Defense Robert McNamara as he was driven into Saigon on October 15, 1965. The guerrilla planted a bomb under a bridge that the motorcade would cross. The ARVN soldiers spotted him when they realized that he was not native to the district, and he was seized and shot. Among the spectators was Nguyen Thi Bao, a Party member who sat in the crowd with the vegetables she had come to sell; it was a momentous day, an experience to be remembered for a lifetime.[2] Troi's young wife, who had married him only days before, agonized as she watched his torture and death, and she herself suffered in jail, but it only convinced her more of the necessity of sacrifice.[3]

The ideological underpinnings of Ho Chi Minh's revolution promised dramatic changes in the lives of women, and they could not be provided by the conservative Saigon government. In the late 1950s, Madame Ngo Dinh Nhu, President Ngo Dinh Diem's sister-in-law and the wife of the head of his secret police and his chief political adviser, attempted to create her own anti-Communist paramilitary women's group to rival the NLF's. The members of the Vietnamese Women's Solidarity Movement, her "little darlings," as she referred to the young women, were outfitted in military garb, trained with weapons, and marched on parade. She herself taught them how to handle pistols. Many were high school and university students who were inspired by her appeals to their morality and promises of a better life for Vietnamese women. She had laws passed outlawing polygamy, divorce, prostitution, and infidelity, which reflected her newfound Catholic faith.[4] Apparently she was amused by her troops' engaging in judo falls on men while marching to a martial tune.[5] In an autocratic regime such as that established by the Ngo brothers in Saigon, young women could not mix on an equal basis with men, let alone accompany them into the field. Imitation may have been the "sincerest form of flattery," but it did not produce equal results.

Preteen children were recruited in ways that suited their ages and corresponded to the experience of their elders. Peasant children received their schooling from the carnage around them and the deaths of family members and friends. They learned to hate foreigners and the government described as their "puppet" as children of the wealthy learned to support their own self-interest. The experience of bombing terrified everyone. A photograph taken on June 8, 1972, by Associated Press photographer Nick Ut of nine-year-old Phan Thi Kim Phuc running naked down a road, the village from which she came burning after a napalm strike that killed her two brothers, turned many Vietnamese against the war, as it did myriad Americans. This graphic image outraged Americans and people around the world, yet for Vietnamese such horrors were not unusual occurrences.[6]

In recruiting children, sometimes the NLF played on their desire for excitement and the Confucian heritage that stressed obedience to parents and duty to family. That the NLF should have recruited children as part of its efforts was not surprising. However, outside observers at first regarded the practice as outrageous, even an act of desperation. Americans found that the use of children in wartime further blurred whatever distinctions remained between this conflict and anything resembling conventional warfare.

Sometimes abandoned infants became helpless pawns, tools of war in a conflict that spared no one. Stories of babies being tied to mines and placed in the middle of roads, thereby posing a terrible dilemma for American soldiers—to run down an infant, or to swerve off the road and into an ambush— became part of the folklore of the Vietnam War, whether true or not. Such tales helped to depersonalize the enemy, to make him or her an inhuman "other," behaving unlike the more "civilized" Americans. Using infants as mines would have been a highly unlikely operating procedure in a culture as family-oriented as Vietnam's. Most tasks were more benign. Participating in health education classes organized by NLF village women was much more practical for NLF youth, who had little access to medical care of any kind.

Older children were active participants in fighting and defense. Children could plant mines, dig traps, carve stakes, and be useful in many ways to help their elders. They also carried messages and acted as guides for the Front forces.[7] If their village was threatened with attack, they as well as their elders gathered intelligence on GVN forces in the area and built primitive defenses, such as *punji* stakes and nailed boards. Boys also participated in sports programs that prepared them to join the guerrilla forces.[8] Girls helped prepare medicines and bandages, and they mended clothing.

In their early teens, many young people joined the Youth Liberation Association, one of the three most significant mass organizations established by the Party. It traced its roots to the Communist Youth League, founded in 1931, but like the associations for farmers and women, it underwent several name changes during the course of the war. But its goals remained the same—to make youths conversant with basic Communist ideology and practice so they could participate in political struggle, and to prepare them to become future guerrillas.[9] They were also taught slogans and stories of past and present heroes. A favorite was that of the Trung sisters, who had led their country to a brief victory over China in C.E. 40. The importance of class (poor peasant, for the most part) was a prominent theme, since it helped youths understand how their families had been exploited by foreigners and the rich. Although the indoctrination was much less intense than that given their elders, the underlying message was the same—resistance. The moral of the Trung sisters, their "desire to pay their debt to the country and to avenge their family," which continued throughout the centuries as a rallying cry, symbolized what young people could do; although the older sister had been married, Trung Nhi was not yet of marriageable age, yet she could be a soldier.[10]

On April 24, 1961, the Youth Liberation Association was formed from the former Communist Youth League, renaming itself as the Women's Liberation Association had done. Its first congress was held in March 1965. Goals were reformulated, plans were made for the future, and the smaller groups of youth who had been part of the resistance in the countryside were praised by the Party for their successes against the Americans. The young men and women were called a "shock army on the battlefield." At the second congress, held on July 1–18, 1973, the Central Committee of the Ho Chi Minh Lao Dong Youth Group sent a telegram of greeting to the youth, terming them a "class of people with 'gold livers and iron intestines' going first and leaving last" and stressed how worthy the young people were of the praise of the deceased but ever venerated Ho Chi Minh. Pham Van Ton, who reported for the youth newspaper *Thanh Nien*, enumerated many acts of heroism by both young men and young women, and emphasized that "female youths have played a key role in the long-haired troops to assist in smashing every plot and strategy of the enemy." Among the many activities he listed were destroying the strategic-hamlet program, defying conscription into the Army of the Republic of Vietnam, and demanding freedom, democracy, and the withdrawal of American troops.[11]

The youths of the association were organized into a number of smaller regional and village groups, just as the adults were, each with its own slogan. Some of these short, catchy phrases showed the activities required of the cell members—for example, the "entire youth group must hold rifles and must be composed of only valiant combatants" and "youth cells and units must be death-defying, spearhead shock forces." About one-third of the membership of the Liberation Youth Union (its name by 1968) consisted of young women. Reports of their activities specifically identified the gender of the membership: "The Phu Yen artillery female units, the Binh Son female cell on detonations, the Gia Lai female cell for attacking communications, and the Que Son female regional forces have, with their outstanding feats-of-arms, glorified the role of the female youths among the armed forces."[12] Membership in such cells gave status to the youths; peer pressure kept them active and helped to alleviate the fear of dying. Even small children learned to contain their dread of the enemy and protect the revolutionaries around them, and they understood the value of silence.

A document from Kien Tuong Province captured in November 1966 stated the goals for the local Alliance Youth Group Committee in less dramatic terminology. The membership was ordered to rally and recruit young people into the youth organizations, indoctrinate them, strengthen their patriotic feelings, deepen their hatred, and urge them to work with the people to carry on the struggle relentlessly and destroy the enemy. The author of the document recognized that many young men were being forced into enlisting in the ARVN, the Regional Forces and Popular Forces, or the Civilian Irregular Defense Group (CIDG). Thus it was even more necessary to convince both male and female youths to "realize their responsibilities and duties of taking up arms to kill the enemy for the country's salvation."[13]

By their mid-teens, many female Youth Liberation Association members were long-haired warriors, fighting with artillery, detonating explosives, and attacking with rifles and other weapons. The story of Hong Quan exemplified the achievements and perils of fighting as part of all-female guerrilla units. She was from a village near Saigon that operated against ARVN forces in the area. Although her unit had many successes, they were surrounded one day and left with only hand grenades with which to defend themselves. Hong Quan was shot in the hand before she could throw her grenade, and she was taken prisoner. Her captors tortured her for information, leaving her wound untreated, and gangrene set in. The enemy brought in her mother, Vo Thi Chi, and tortured her in front of her wounded daughter in an effort to get names of other Communists in the unit. This tactic, to torture one family member in order to force another one to reveal names, was standard practice that often worked among families with strong loyalties and Confucian values. The revolutionaries referred to it as mental torture, which was then combined with physical torture to obtain the desired result. Seeing your mother beaten was worse than being maltreated yourself. However, Hong Quan refused to recognize Chi as her mother, and she was not moved when the guards accused her of being a bad daughter, not caring for her mother. The mother likewise refused to recognize Quan as her daughter, even when the wounded young woman was tortured in front of her eyes. Finally, the ARVN captors gave up, amputated Quan's lower arm, but continued abusing her. She and her mother remained stalwart, however, and neither one talked. After the war, they moved to Saigon, where their family bonds were stronger than ever.[14]

Poetry was used to create models of behavior for youth to emulate. Tales of young women who attacked without fear, withstood torture, and, despite terrible suffering, continued to fight without betraying their comrades were passed along to other youth groups as examples to follow, and many years later they were still recalled by women in the Vietnam Women's Union. At the office of the union in Hue, the women described the heroism of a young woman called only "Miss Hoa," who during the war had worked as a messenger. When the enemy caught her, they took off her clothes and paraded her nude through the village for seven days, which was extremely humiliating for Vietnamese women, who valued modesty. The Saigon soldiers were angered when she refused to give them information, so they cut off her breasts and stuck things up her vagina. She said to them that they could not stop her love for her country and the revolution. She knew she was going to die, but it was an honor to do so for her country. She then bit off her tongue so she could not speak.[15]

Young women in their late teens undertook a variety of tasks. Those young women who transported goods carried out heavy physical labor, yet gender was no barrier to performance. As their bodies became accustomed to more weight, they carried ever heavier loads up and down hills and across streams. After some months, these teenagers, whose weight was probably not even 100 pounds, could carry that much or more. After the war, women reminiscing about their exploits could not believe they had carried such heavy loads, especially as they were often ill and malnourished. Mundane work such as typing reports, distributing leaflets, gathering information on the location of the enemy, and transporting food up the rivers of the South by sampan were also essential to the survival of the Front. They and their mothers passed along information at the markets—marketing was women's work, gossiping a traditional pastime—and it was hard for outsiders to determine what was being said. These "market mouths," as they were called, were very useful in intelligence work. If the youths were successful, they might one day become members of the Communist Party. But the Party was very selective, and few would achieve that goal.

One area in which youths excelled was espionage. Recruiting of students for espionage was taking place in Military Region 1, which included Saigon. Young people had long been useful in demonstrations against local governments because they could so easily be mobilized. By 1970, professors and students were arrested and imprisoned in all the major prisons of the South, and even young children and the old were deported to the island prison of Con Dao.[16] An enemy document captured in February 1974 revealed an amazing tale of the intended formation of the Trung Duong Poetical and Literary Group among elementary and high-school students in Saigon. A monk, Thich Thien Luan, organized a meeting for four high-school students, telling them that the name was a cover for a proposed espionage group of boys and girls. They were to collect any "military, political, and social information discussed at home among family members, especially information concerning the activities of GVN security agencies." They were to identify themselves by embroidering the letters "NBTN" (unity of the South and North) on the hems of the back of the boys' shirts and the hems of the girls' dresses. He went on to describe how they were to be divided into a central group, cells, chapters, general chapters, and subchapters. The top members were eligible to join the Party if they did their job well and were sponsored by two Party members. The monk, in reality a Communist cadre named Le Van Hao, told them that they did not have to worry about being brutalized by the police if they were arrested because they were under age eighteen.

They would undergo only two months of "political reorientation" and then be released. Although Hao's operation was nipped in the bud, the American adviser who investigated this case noted that such activities might well have been operating in other schools to indoctrinate students into "VC operations." [17]

The lives of many Communist women demonstrate how childhood involvement grew to a lifelong commitment. Nguyen Thi Dung of the village of Dinh Thuy in Ben Tre Province described how participation in the Youth Liberation Association had led her to membership in the Women's Liberation Association and lifelong involvement in the activities of the NLF and the Party. She said that she had participated in revolutionary activities since 1962 when she was a child, had joined the Youth Liberation Association in 1965, and immediately had helped organize demonstrations. She was attracted to Communist ideology and hated foreign oppressors who kept her people poor. She followed the Party's orders and became a member in 1968. For her, participating was part of her family's and village's tradition, and her youth was no liability.[18] Ngo Thi Bich Loi, from a village near Hue, was the only child of a revolutionary family. She joined the resistance movement in 1964, when she was fourteen years old, distributing leaflets and gathering news of the enemy. She helped guerrillas hide in her house until she was recognized by the enemy and was ordered to go to the "resistance area," the jungle, to be safe.[19]

Given the nature of the Vietnam War, the recruitment of children made ideological sense and was a reasonable effort to ensure future members of the NLF. However, it did lead to ideological splits in families, as some young women sided with the guerrillas and young men, sometimes their brothers, were drafted by the ARVN. Le Ly Hayslip's story, *When Heaven and Earth Changed Places,* and Yung Krall's memoir, *A Thousand Tears Falling,* are poignant accounts of the way the war pulled families apart and set brother fighting brother.[20] Young women might be further conflicted if romance interfered with ideology.

Children were trained for membership in the revolution in several ways. Most followed the path of family members and other influential adults in their village, since they remained in their home region throughout their lives. But there were notable exceptions, even among young women. Some were the

children of "stay-behinds" or were "stay-behinds" themselves. They had
been instructed by the Party to remain in the South when Vietnam was divided in 1954 in compliance with the Geneva Accords. Some "stay-behinds"
were young people who had specific tasks or reasons to linger. Ca Le Du of
the village of Dinh Thuy remained because she was engaged to be married
to a revolutionary. Older teenagers who were ordered to stay were considered by the Party to be important and useful in their own right.

Two groups of young people went north after the exchange of populations. Some children, offspring of important Party members in the South,
went to the North to study or be trained, and some even traveled as far as
Moscow and East European nations for higher education. They would be
the future elite of the revolutionary state. Many of these young people came
from families that had fought with the Viet Minh during World War II against
the Japanese, and continued to resist the French after the end of the Pacific
War. Others had revolutionary pedigrees dating even earlier than that; they
descended from families that had been members of the Indochinese Communist Party since the 1930s.

My guide and translator in Ho Chi Minh City, who used the pseudonym
Nguyen Thi Sau, had been such a child. Her father had been ordered to the
North in 1950 to fight the French in the battle of Bien Gioi on the border of
Vietnam and China. The family suffered political persecution and fled to
the jungle; after 1954, they moved to the North. Sau, the youngest, stayed
behind, but later was sent to Hanoi along the Trail: to her, it was the Truong
Son; to the Americans, it would be the Ho Chi Minh. Traveling to Hanoi
by foot and bus took several months and was a perilous journey. She at-
tended school in Hanoi, where she and other children from the South were
considered "special children" by Uncle Ho, who told them they were his
own; this alleviated the homesickness they felt. Ho Chi Minh visited their
school, where Sau and the other young girls danced for him, a memory that
has stayed with Sau.[21]

By 1965, when American forces entered the war in great numbers and
the first bombing raids of the North, Operation Rolling Thunder, began,
families already separated had to make painful decisions about where to stay
during what promised to be a long conflict. Some parents had gone to the
North in 1954 when the Geneva Accords had called for the regrouping of
Communists above the seventeenth parallel, and they had left small children behind with grandparents. Some of these children went north at this

time, as did others, who were sent to Hanoi so they could be educated under a Communist system and, if they qualified, sent to the Soviet bloc for higher education.

Nguyen Thi Tinh went to Hanoi when her parents, former Viet Minh and then NLF members, decided that she should have a proper socialist education. She was educated there, and then traveled to several Soviet bloc countries to study foreign languages. In Cuba, she learned both English and Spanish. She returned to Hanoi in the late 1970s, by which time her linguistic abilities were very useful. She preferred living in the North and was allowed by the Party to marry and remain there.[22] She found Hanoi ideologically purer than Saigon, which remained somewhat decadent even after its reincarnation as Ho Chi Minh City.

Another girl, Tran Thi Ly, from a peasant family in Go Noi village, Quang Nam Province, joined the guerrillas at the age of nine during the war against France. Her father died when she was very young, and the large family lived in dire poverty. As young as she was, she worked with the Women's Liberation Association in her village and then at the district level. Ly was arrested by the French, but freed when the First Indochina War ended. After the Geneva Accords, the Party ordered her to remain in the South and continue her revolutionary activity. Now a teenager, she became a secret messenger for the Central Committee of the Communist Party of her district until she was captured by the ARVN while delivering a petition from her fellow villagers to the GVN authorities in Da Nang; it demanded that the terms of the Geneva Accords be met. She had been arrested twice before but released for lack of evidence. But the documents and the villagers' petition convinced the GVN officials that she was a member of the NLF. At this point, her story became legendary. Although she was beaten for months, she was still able to cry out to a female comrade next to her, "Clench your teeth, sister, and you'll feel less hurt." When her captors could not succeed in getting her to reveal information, they called her a Viet Cong slut and dropped their bamboo canes.[23] She was sent from prison to prison and finally back to Da Nang. When her captors thought that she was nearly dead, they threw her into the road, where her comrades found her and nursed her back to life. She received medical attention in Da Nang, and then was taken to Cambodia to rest and recover. Next she was moved to Hanoi and later to the Soviet Union, East Germany, and Poland for further medical care. Her wounds were so horrifying that she received extensive publicity in the socialist world: red-hot steel rods had been thrust up her vagina, and she continued to bleed despite medical care. She had continual headaches from the beatings, and remained hospitalized or bedridden for the rest of her life. The Party gave permission for her to marry a man from Da Nang, who related her life story to all who visited the house where she had died. He said that they had met when they were both patients in the Hanoi hospital. Unable to have children, they adopted a little girl. As Ly lay dying of cancer, she asked her husband to gather her possessions and make a shrine at their home, with a large picture of her when she was young and beautiful at its center. He said that many well-known Party officials—Pham Van Dong, Le Duan, Madame Nguyen Thi Binh, and Le Duc Tho—had visited her in her last days. After her death in 1992, the shrine became a memorial to her contributions to the Communist cause, for her bravery and courage led to her becoming a heroine throughout the socialist world. She acquired faith in Communism as a young child, and she never lost it.[24]

Ly's story, like those of so many others, was a powerful emulation tale that elicited strong emotions over the barbarity of the enemy. But its historical significance documented not only her bravery but the young age at which she became active in the women's movement. She joined at age nine, probably becoming a Young Pioneer, and then, at fourteen, a member of the Ho Chi Minh Youth Association (a special group in the Youth Liberation Association). She symbolized perseverance, the ability to withstand great suffering without breaking down and revealing anything to the enemy. That she was ordered to be a "stay-behind" in 1954 indicated that she was already extremely valuable to the Party, capable of following orders without betraying her comrades if she was caught and tortured. The Communists did treat men and women equally, and women were valued for their ability to suffer silently. Ly came from the poor-peasant class and lived in poverty, which must have helped to qualify her as a Party member. Her background, her actions, and her suffering made her life valuable in Party annals. It also demonstrated the particular resilience and ability to resist that women possessed.

The Youth Liberation Association proselytized to gain recruits for the People's Liberation Armed Forces and the guerrillas and to get young people to work as laborers on the front lines. In 1969, in a speech from Hanoi via Liberation Radio, the broadcaster said that in all liberated areas of central Vietnam, the Vietnamese Youth Liberation Association had been very successful. In Ben Tre, more than 500 youths had joined the PLAF, over 450 sided with the guerrillas, some 1,650 were laborers, and more than 600 had joined the uprising forces. In An Giang Province, more than 100 youths from the Hoa Hao sect, as well as members of other minority religions, had joined the revolutionaries. The report gave no breakdown on the number of young men and young women; probably it was about one-third women, the usual statistic cited elsewhere. If these impressive statistics are to be believed, the proselytizing had an effect, however temporary, on young people.[25]

That young children could be persuaded or recruited through emotions into the youth groups was quickly realized by the People's Revolutionary Party and the NLF. In an article for *Vietnam Feature Service,* a journalist, writing for supporters of the South Vietnamese government, expressed disgust over the use of children as terrorists. The writer described the assassination of a GVN hamlet chief in Binh Dinh Province on March 13, 1970. A Popular Forces platoon pursued the suspects and captured a sixteen-year-old girl and a thirteen-year-old boy. "Increasingly the communists are showing themselves willing and eager to use juveniles for any assignment no matter how grisly," the journalist editorialized, noting that youths were used for "any assignment from sabotage to mass murder." This was attributed to the young people's "yearning for adventure and thrills." This paragraph referred to male teenagers, and the author noted that some 70 percent of Viet Cong saboteurs in Saigon were boys twelve to fifteen years old.[26] However, as the story itself indicates, young women were also assassins, and could have been even more useful because they seemed such unlikely killers.

The actions of revolutionary youth could be interpreted as effective terrorist and violent deeds of fanatic Communist-inspired young people or, conversely, as signs of desperation that showed Communism to be on its last legs. The North regarded deadly violence carried out by young women in particular as worthy of emulation. Violence carried out by female youths was often as deadly as that of young males. To the North, their work was commendable. The Hanoi newspaper *Nhan Dan* printed a speech given by Nguyen Thi Rao on March 8, 1969, regarding the actions of both young and old who became "kill-American" heroes. She praised the work of a fifteen-year-old girl named Bui Thi Hien from Long An Province, south of Saigon, who "singlehandedly implanted a mine and destroyed an American mechanized vehicle."[27] An article in the *Liberation Press* from the Central Region People's Revolutionary Youth Group praised the efforts of "Youth Group female member Nguyen Thi Be, in Binh Dinh province, [who] was captured and barbarously tortured by the enemy three times in three waves

. . . .

of struggle against the enemy. Nevertheless, she was constantly seen taking the lead in the ensuing waves of struggle."[28]

Such violence was viewed by at least one Saigon journalist as a sign that the NLF was weak, even nearing collapse. This writer saw these children as the dregs of society, trained to be cannon fodder. Writing in January 1970, the observer said that these youths were from seven to seventeen years old. They were to be drilled "as guerrillas, sappers, political cadres, spies and terrorists." No longer the offspring of the elite, many came from the dregs of society—the homeless, refugees, and orphans. The NLF was "taking any child they can lay their hands on," the writer said. Since the NLF recognized that the war would be drawn out, it "prepared for the future by recruiting the young." Most were from age ten to seventeen, but many were children younger than ten years of age. The source of this information, a defector from the NLF, noted that the children carried small bundles as they marched north along the Ho Chi Minh Trail. Approximately 30 percent were female, and all the children appeared to be in good health. The children were accompanied by cadre who had led troops to the South; these seasoned veterans were too old or sick to labor or fight any more.[29] This article, written about six months after the previous paean, captured a bit of reality. By 1970, the war was a long-drawn-out struggle, and recruits of any age were a necessity. The United States had begun to withdraw its troops in June 1969, which forced the GVN to use more of its own young people, while the PAVN and the PLAF recruited steadily during the duration of the conflict in the attempt each waged to win the war of attrition.

Suicide cells were organized in late 1967 to prepare for the general offensive planned for Tet of January 1968. They were three-person units whose task was to eliminate "tyrants," "spies," and GVN police. The squads were formed at the village level and often consisted of teenagers. In one district of Binh Dinh Province, each village was ordered by the NLF to establish a "suicide unit" with from ten to twenty male and female members, fifteen years or older, that would then be broken down into three-person cells. The unit's task was to kill so-called traitors, ARVN Special Forces, pacification personnel, and rural development officials. Many teams at least attempted this. During Tet, the units inflicted many casualties; the NLF apparently had intended to assassinate even more people than it was able to do. The lack of sufficient personnel, inadequate information on the addresses of targets, the inexperience of the suicide cells' members, the dearth of weapons, and even an unwillingness to fight prevented greater damage to the GVN and its foreign supporters.[30] Assassination teams worked throughout the war to terrorize villagers in the South to support the NLF, but the suicide squads differed in their willingness to sacrifice their own lives.

Some young people did become very effective killers. Once they had joined the Youth Liberation Association, the most promising were recruited to volunteer for suicidal terrorist attack cells called "determined to die." Their willingness to sacrifice themselves was intensified through classic Marxist-Leninist techniques, with stimulation of class hatred, loathing for the American "imperialists" and their "lackeys" in Saigon, and self-criticism.[31] Recruitment was encouraged by the village cadre, who was to assign "volunteers" to each cell, some of whom were ordered to be leaders. Membership consisted of male and female youths and older men and women. The members participated in an oath-taking ceremony before the people of the hamlet, but only the names of those in two of the cells were introduced. The total number of cells in a hamlet was revealed, not the members' names. After the oath-taking, a tea ceremony was held so that members could swear to carry out their tasks.[32]

A female Vietnamese psychologist, Tang Thi Thanh Van, who interviewed a number of young *chieu hoi*, described her talks with a twelve-year-old boy who had been working with an assassination squad. She said that he had killed six South Vietnamese combat policemen and one American soldier during the offensive in May 1968. He was not bothered by the killing, he told her, but he was afraid of being spanked by his parents when he went home. She commented that the children were usually nonpolitical and joined the units in the hope of receiving their own gun.[33]

As the war continued, more emphasis was placed on the recruitment of youth. In 1970, a report, probably from the Party committee in Binh Dinh, urged the establishment of combat hamlets (armed and ready to defend themselves against ARVN forces) and villages in lowland and mountainous areas; the initiation of a youth enlistment movement to reinforce guerrilla and main force units was ordered. The recruiting of youth was necessary in the fighting of protracted war, since a new generation could replace the old.[34]

Other documents had a tone of desperation as they discussed the use of children. For example, "iron bulwark children" was a title created in 1970 to be awarded to children who served the revolutionary cause in exemplary ways. These youngsters were to undertake activities such as the

collection of dud bombs and ammunition, the destruction of enemy propaganda leaflets, and the obstruction of other pro-NLF activities in their
local areas. The orders, probably issued by the Youth Proselyting Section
of a subregion of COSVN, indicated the need to bring people of any age
and either sex into the Front. The mottos to be learned were similar to
those used for adults; the cadre were to urge children to "obey Uncle
Ho's . . . five teachings for children, to do a small task as a contribution to
victories over the Americans."[35] The five teachings were to study hard the
words of Communism, work hard, maintain solidarity with their group
(which meant that they were not to fight with one another), maintain good
discipline, and observe good sanitation.[36]

The most direct contact that youths had with adults who could supervise
them and guide them into the Party was through the Women's Liberation
Association. Although the Farmer's Liberation Association was the most
important of the mass groups, women had closer ties to children and young
people because they were related by kinship groups and friendships. Although men joined the NLF and were sent to the jungles, women with
large families remained in their villages.[37] An important document, dated
April 1968, stated that women of the liberation associations were to "ur-
gently coordinate with the youths, educate and motivate young men and
women to join the Assault Youth Movement in accordance with the guidance and instructions laid down by the Youth Group."[38] Teenagers and
young adults were needed to participate in radical actions against the
enemy.[39]

The NLF recruited not only Vietnamese youth, but also tribal young people
from the mountains. Sometimes its efforts met with success. Nong Thi Trung
of the Tay national minority had "followed Uncle Ho's advice and taken
part in the struggle." She had won the right to have her own land or to have
an education and equality. Naturally, she chose the latter. Trung, "like her
many sisters throughout the country, had come to know the revolution during
the most difficult years." This young woman, from a tribe in the North, had
seen the success of the August Revolution of 1945 and had fought against
the French. Now she could have liberty and equality.[40]

While minority women in the South were mentioned in emulation documents for people of that region, they were less likely recruits than those in
the North. American military personnel did recruit them and were often

successful, since they could play on their hatred of the ethnic Vietnamese. Sometimes they were willing to engage in kinds of violence that Americans eschewed.[41]

By the last few years of the war, the populace—men, women, and children—was exhausted. The doctrinaire Communists continued the resistance, but there was a movement for peace. Unfortunately for the government of Vietnam, the American government, exhausted by the cost of the long war and the lack of support of the American public, chose to withdraw. This left the North and South to fight it out between themselves.

6

• • • • • • • • • • • • • • • •

WAR IN THE NORTH

Just as certain photographic images from the conflict in the South aroused the American conscience about the war—a monk aflame in a Saigon intersection; a young girl, Kim Phuc, running down the road burning with napalm; a Saigon police chief shooting a Viet Cong suspect in the head during the Tet offensive—some images captured the war in the North as well. They received worldwide publicity and dramatized the destructiveness of the conflict and the inequities that the high-tech American war brought to a peasant society. Many well-known shots showed peasants armed, aiming at the sky and defending their villages as well as Hanoi and other cities of the North. Ho Chi Minh's kindly character was also a subject of photographs: the famous picture of him seated on the steps as little children ran to him for his loving embrace captured his supposed fatherly character, while pictures of the destruction of the Bach Mai hospital in Hanoi during the Christmas bombing of 1972 dramatized the inhumanity of the Americans. Images of people grieving at the news of Ho Chi Minh's death captured the strong sentiments they felt for Uncle Ho.

Perhaps the best-known picture from the North was that of a small peasant woman, Nguyen Thi Kim Lai, the head of a female militia unit in Huong Khue District who was just seventeen years old, aiming a large rifle at a very large American soldier, Captain William Robinson, age twenty-two, who had been shot down during the Christmas bombing of Hanoi in 1972. Kim Lai led him out of the jungle to Hoa Lo Prison, called by Americans the Hanoi Hilton. The photograph is symbolic of the war in many ways: the girl could handle a rifle, defend her village, and till her family's fields. The war came to her as it came to many in the South—from the skies, from planes whose pilots dropped bombs on the countryside, on small villages, and on the cities of Hanoi, Haiphong, and Vinh. The picture of the girl with her prisoner was reproduced around the world, and even was printed on postage stamps. It symbolized well the relative size of the two antagonists, the unfairness of the conflict, the determination of the Communists to win, and the power of women.[1]

The story had a dramatic ending. Robinson, like many American servicemen, returned to Vietnam, and in May 1985, he met Kim Lai in Hanoi. He asked her forgiveness for his attempt to destroy her village, and she willingly gave it.

After the French war and the Geneva Accords of 1954, the Democratic Republic of Vietnam enjoyed a decade of relative peace before conflict with the United States became a full-scale war. In reality, men had been infiltrated south along the Ho Chi Minh Trail since 1959, and Hanoi had been preparing for conflict. Women served the revolutionary cause from the 1930s on. Female guerrillas supported and aided the Viet Minh opposition to the French, and they suffered heavily in the Japanese occupation during World War II. The Vichy French collaborators with the Japanese occupation aided policies that hurt women, children, and the old disproportionately; during the famine of 1944, primarily the result of Japanese policies that forced peasants to raise jute instead of food crops, they were the first victims.[2]

Vo Nguyen Giap, selected by Ho Chi Minh to organize an army out of the Viet Minh, formed a band of thirty-four guerrillas, three of whom were women. Their first action, taken at the end of 1944, was to seize a French outpost; they killed the commander and took the arsenal, and then raided another fort fifteen miles away, killing two officers. These events have been described by journalist-historian Stanley Karnow as the beginnings of the Vietnamese army.[3]

During the French war, however, most women carried out other activities. They were skilled at gathering intelligence, liaising, providing food, and assisting the army with sustenance and munitions. At the battle of Dien Bien Phu in the winter and spring of 1953/1954, women hauled supplies over the mountains for the troops of General Giap. They shouldered tremendous burdens, carrying foodstuffs, ammunition, even artillery pieces, with little assistance except for ropes, mules, or bicycles. Most were minority women, enlisted by Giap from the nearby villages. The general found that they were a more reliable workforce than the men.[4] Minority people were not easy to convert to Communism; they were distrustful of the Vietnamese and disinterested in ideology. By promising autonomy in an eventually independent Vietnam under Communism, Ho and Giap recruited from the Hmong, the Thai, and the Tho. Karnow wrote that the cadres "trekked through the area [northern Vietnam] like itinerant missionaries, holding meetings, preaching salvation and creating cells, each composed of five men and women whose job was to convert other villagers to the cause."[5] Women not only proselytized and recruited, but acted as intelligence agents and even fought in guerrilla units.[6] But the war against France was only the latest step in arousing in northern women the spirit of resistance.

Women in urban and rural areas of the North lived traditional lives, more bound to Confucian strictures than their southern sisters because they had absorbed more Chinese influence. In families where a man could afford to support more than one woman, several wives and many concubines vied for his attention. Women were usually illiterate and bound to the home. They often became the helpless victims of French rapaciousness and violence. During the French War, Bui Tin, who would become a prominent military officer in the People's Army of Viet Nam, taught local people how to conduct ambushes, lay mines, and sabotage French railroads. He hated the French because they had shot his mother; her only crime was being married to his father, who had been a high-ranking Viet Minh official.[7]

Ideas of independence circulated in Hanoi in the 1920s and 1930s, some based on reform, others on revolution. To engage in political activity was illegal under French law, and the punishment for those caught was harsh, so talk had to be circumspect. To discuss the role of women provided a nice cover for discussing structural changes in society, but such talk did not convert either men or women to the Communist ideology. Male writers were more concerned with discussing women-as-victims, suffering under the traditional obligations of pleasing their husbands and mothers-in-law, than in viewing females as potential radicals. Those few women who were Marxist, like Nguyen Thi Minh Khai, were not necessarily feminists either: she regarded women's struggles as subordinate to the larger issues of class conflict.[8] Women could be of little use to the revolution unless they were educated. Of those who did learn to read, few went beyond three years of schooling unless their fathers had taught them at home. Most of the literate could make out individual words on a blackboard, but could not read books or pamphlets. The rest of their radicalization came from oral memorization. Of course, not all who received this cursory schooling became Communists; many others chose paths for advancement other than Communism or any political ideology.[9] There was no natural affinity between feminism and Communism. Much of the radical tradition drew on the concept of the victimized woman who needed to be helped, not on woman as a force for liberation and equal participant in the class struggle.

The creation of the organization that would become Vietnam Women's Union followed the pattern that Ho Chi Minh had established for the creation of mass organizations. The organization of women went through many name changes from its founding in 1930 as the Women's Emancipation Association. It was variously the Women's Democratic Association (1936–1939), the Women's Anti-Colonialist Association (1939–1941), and the Women's Association for National Salvation (June 1941–November 20, 1946). At that time, its name was changed to the Vietnam Women's Union, the name it retained throughout the wars and afterward. The Women's Union differed from the Women's Liberation Association in that the Women's Union existed as an agency of the Communist Party in a Communist state. The Women's Liberation Association, however, was affiliated with the National Liberation Front. It was Communist-dominated, but it included other patriotic groups that were united in their hatred of the Saigon regimes and the American invaders. The Women's Liberation Association and its many branches theoretically received their instructions from Hanoi, but due to the exigencies of war, they operated in a more independent fashion. The two groups were united in 1975 when the North and South were merged into one country. The president of the Women's Union from 1955 to 1975 was Nguyen Thi Thap; she was succeeded by Nguyen Thi Dinh.[10]

From its founding, the Vietnam Women's Union held congresses, first in 1950, then in 1956, then in 1961. It held a twenty-year anniversary in 1966, celebrating the official beginning of the union in 1946. Representatives from the North and South were included in the union and participated in the congresses, but in 1961 a separate organization, the South Vietnam Women's Liberation Association, was formed, targeted specifically against "US imperialism." The presidents of the Women's Liberation Association were Nguyen Thi Cam Tu, who served from 1963 to 1968, and Nguyen Thi Dinh, who became president of the united organization in 1976.[11]

At congresses held on the average of one every five years, plans were made for the next targeted period. The Communist Party and the leaders of the Women's Union praised the achievements of women, especially those in the South. The leaders told stories of heroines to encourage the delegates to emulate them and to push members of their village associations toward greater sacrifices. The women held self-criticism sessions to identify and rectify errors they had made and to stimulate more recruiting into the ranks. Often the meetings coincided with March 8, International Women's Day, and greetings were read from women in other socialist bloc countries. Sometimes a short statement was delivered by Madame Nguyen Thi Binh, who traveled to many Third World countries as a representative of the People's Revolutionary Government of South Vietnam. Nguyen Thi Dinh also sent messages of encouragement.

Northern women hated the bondage of colonialism, but victory over the French promised them a change in their lives. However, they found that their goals had to be deferred to those of society at large. Ho Chi Minh pledged them a utopia in the 1946 constitution and in his words of equality. But independence came first, and even when it had been won, men were reluctant to consider women their equals. Afterward, the entire populace had to recover from the destruction wrought by the war against France. This task had to be undertaken very carefully to avoid alienating the more moderate elements of society, since the Viet Minh was a nationalist, not exclusively Communist, organization. After recovery, Hanoi's goal was the construction of a socialist society, again taking great care since this could alienate all but the poorest people in the country. The final goal, independence from the intervention of the United States and its "puppets" in Saigon, had to proceed along with the reunification of the country—the next and symbolically most important goal. Women had to sublimate their aspirations to these goals and hope that the final victory would bring liberation for them as well.

Many women participated in the combat against France and shared in the creation of a socialist society in the North, but not all reaped the rewards of their sacrifice. Bui Tin, a defector from the North after the war, told the story of one woman, Nguyen Thi Nam, who had helped the revolutionaries as far back as 1937. Her two sons joined the Viet Minh and were, by 1954, officers; she also sheltered revolutionaries in her home. Yet during the land reforms, the local Chinese adviser concluded that she was a cruel landlord who must be eliminated. The case was brought to Ho Chi Minh himself, who, according to Tin, dared not intervene against the Chinese adviser, nor did Party Secretary Truong Chinh. Nguyen Thi Nam was killed.[12] She was not the only innocent victim.

The period of land reform in the late 1950s had two aspects: on the one hand, many people were unjustly labeled large landholders and lost their land. On the other, although land distribution brought great hardship and sometimes death for many people, there may have been something positive for a few women.[13] Those who had supported the fight for independence from the French were encouraged to take leadership roles in the reconstruction of society. Cadres showed women how to plant new varieties of seeds and use different fertilizers, and female peasants participated in the distribution of land and collectivization of agriculture.[14] The defeat of France had brought a weakening of the age-old Confucian patterns of inferiority and the first indication that real equality for women might be realized. However, the issue of class struggle, a fundamental tenet of Marxism-Leninism and thus of Ho Chi Minh's belief system, was still posed against the concept of gender equality.

When the American war began, the women of the Democratic Republic of Vietnam responded with alacrity to Hanoi's call to resist the aggressors, aid their southern brethren, and ultimately achieve unification. Given the nature of the North's authoritarian regime, they had little choice, but one must not underestimate the powerful effect of propaganda, which stressed the similarity of this conflict to the French war—the nation again attacked by a foreign invader determined to eliminate its independence—and the potential loss of their husbands, sons, brothers, and sweethearts. To the North and the South, Vietnam was one country made up of one people, and attempts to create a new state south of an arbitrary dividing line were a perversion of history. Propaganda calling the Saigon government a puppet regime installed and controlled by the United States was easy to sell, for its new backers, the Americans, were primarily Caucasian, as were the former French overlords. Northern women had no more desire than their southern sisters to lose their men to a new conflict, but the North pledged itself to a protracted war, to wear down an enemy of vastly superior strength and technology. When the Americans began bombing the North in 1964, hatred of an enemy that rained death from the skies was well-nigh universal.

Organized into chapters of the Women's Union, northern women of all ages reacted to the same propaganda as was used in the South. Young Volunteers' Brigades, the counterpart of the Youth Liberation Association in the South, transported supplies to the front and repaired roads damaged by bombing; although most of the volunteers were male, some female or mixed units were created. One group of ten young women who were about seventeen years old was stationed at Dong Loc, near the border of the North and South at a major intersection of a road going into Laos from the North. They marched along the road to help truck drivers find their way in the dark, and they helped defend the crossing. They wore white shirts and black pants, and the reflection of moonlight off their shirts guided the drivers. On July 24, 1968, they were all killed when a bomb from an American raid struck their bunker. They were awarded the "Hero Unit" citation posthumously, and the story of their tragic deaths became another source of inspiration to emulate.[15]

In 1965, the Central Committee of the Vietnam Women's Union devised the "three responsibilities" movement, with paradigms to instruct women about their wartime duties.[16] They were ordered to take their husband's places in the fields, maintaining agricultural production so that the men could go south to fight. They were to care for their families, raising their children for the cause of the revolution and conducting family affairs. They were to go to the fields with hoe in one hand, rifle in the other, to till the soil and defend their villages from invasion or attack from the skies. It was expected that they also would encourage their sons and husbands to join the army and fight, sacrificing personal happiness for the fatherland and the revolution.[17] Urban and rural women, even members of minority tribes, were trained to defend their land and to honor their southern sisters, who were sacrificing even more because the enemy lived among them. In a sense, as Lady Borton has said, the northern women were more truly long-haired warriors than their southern sisters: they were the home guard to patrol their villages and warn their neighbors in case of aerial attack, and they even had to defend Hanoi during the American bombing campaigns: Linebacker I and II.[18] They learned to fire Chinese weapons and Soviet anti-aircraft guns. They were heroic in the manner of the Trung sisters, and they were inspired not only by love of country but by Communist ideology.

The basic principles of the three responsibilities applied to peasant women, but all women had tasks to do. As Le Thi Nham Tuyet wrote, using appropriate Communist rhetoric, it was a "vivid illustration of the communion between the will of the Government and the Party and the wishes of the people, of their determination to fight."[19] Women's labors during the American war were far different from those during the French war; they faced a much stronger enemy, so they had to work and study harder, learning to do tasks they had never done before and increasing their own strength. Rural women learned techniques for raising rice and did heavy agricultural labor, such as plowing with oxen or water buffalo. Eventually, women augmented the production of rice to five or seven tons of rice per hectare (two and a half acres), obtaining two or sometimes three crops a year. They also learned to raise cotton, potatoes, jute, soybeans, cassava, peanuts, sugar cane, and tea. They were primarily responsible for supplying soldiers with food, but they also had to feed the urban population.[20]

Other women carried out their own version of the three responsibilities. Industrial workers had "one hand with hammer, one hand with gun," while intellectuals had "one hand with pen, one hand with gun." Tuyet described other tasks they performed. They camouflaged anti-aircraft guns with branches and leaves, and they "used straw to make hats and bulletproof coats for the military." Women also "supplied food and drink to the battle front, [and] carried wounded soldiers home and returned them to their units after recovery." They helped soldiers hide from the bombs, gave them medical assistance, collected baskets of unexploded bombs on rice fields, destroyed slow-exploding bombs, and served on ferries to transport soldiers across the rivers while they were attacked by bombs and shells and torpedo boats were nearby.[21]

Nguyen Thi Xuot, known as Mother Suot, was an impoverished peasant who had been a virtual slave during the French colonial period. She married, but her husband left her for another woman, and her sons were taken by the wars. During the First Indochina War, she ferried revolutionary soldiers across a river by boat. By 1964, she was making her living at the Nhat Le River, taking people and provisions across. By February 1965, she had begun to serve in the war against the Americans, again using her boat. This time, she carried bullets to anti-aircraft guns in the camp of the People's Army of Vietnam. Many bombs fell as she did her duty, but she was not deterred. She became a symbol of the Vietnamese mother serving her country during wartime. In 1967, she was awarded the title Hero of Labor by President Ho Chi Minh.[22]

Women were formed into female militia units, to be in charge of defending bridges and roads, shooting at planes, and fighting South Vietnamese Rangers near the boundary of North and South. The militia and self-defense forces were trained in the use of weapons, especially anti-aircraft guns. Although they were not permitted to go south until 1966, women did work in transportation teams to carry food supplies as far as they were allowed to travel, hauling ammunition and weapons as well. They trained for and participated in assault teams that were prepared to fight if the country was invaded. Inspired by the three responsibilities movement, they provided munitions to air-defense units under attack. One captured male soldier from the PAVN reported that the women's morale was high and that the Party had told them the Americans had brought about the war, which was becoming bloodier every day. If they had any complaints, he said, it was that they were not allowed to go south to fight.[23] To them, liberating the South was a sacred mission.

As the war intensified, all young women were required to join the local militia and self-defense units, making up 41 percent of the total and augmenting old people and those unable to fight in the South. By 1969, women were allowed to join the army, and some were highly decorated.[24] Fighting in the South was considered an honor, at least until reality set in. Duong Thu Huong's account, *Novel Without a Name*, although about a young male soldier, was apparently based on her own experiences as a leader in the Communist Youth Brigade, and they were horrifying, not glamorous.[25]

Women workers in the North, like those in the South, were exposed to emulation campaigns, where they were told stories of particularly brave women after whom they should model themselves. One story told of a woman who pushed a cart full of rice for twenty-five miles along a muddy road, husked and pounded it, and then transported it back to her work site, where there was a food shortage. Another "woman hero" could not rest or eat if there was a pothole to be filled on the road; she would work all night to repair them. Another woman managed to care for her small child while turning out a record amount of cloth at her factory.[26] Such tales, which often verged on the unreal, were standard repertoire in Communist storytelling.

Women also performed more skilled and specialized work. They replaced men as physicians and public-health personnel, jobs that only a few women had held before the war. By 1969, women composed 33 percent of skilled workers and scientific cadres. Altogether, women became 60 to 80 percent of the workforce in the North, laboring in the fields, factories, and offices.[27] They also taught in universities and worked for the government.

The care of children sent to the countryside to save them from the bombing attacks also fell to the women. The children's parents were involved in war work, but the children needed care and schooling, and members of the Women's Union were assigned to help. Vuong Thi Hanh described how she had evacuated a group of children from Hanoi, hid them in a cave, and taught them. She said her only problem was keeping them indoors when bombs began to fall in the distance. The children wanted to see the airplanes and smoke, and they did not realize that the planes could harm them. Women also had to block the entrances to the caves with their bodies during bombing raids to shield the children from shrapnel, and to care for those who became orphaned.[28] Sometimes the women themselves were killed while protecting their charges. Ngo Thi Chuc cared for small children outside Hanoi. When the bombers came, she took the children into bomb shelters. After the attack, she went outside to make sure they were safe and was killed when a delayed-action bomb exploded in front of the shelter. The children survived.[29]

Women who remembered their experiences as children during the attacks on Hanoi have vivid memories to this day. Nguyen Thi Phuong recalled that all the children were instructed in first aid, so they could care for themselves if they were caught in a bombing raid. Phuong was just nine when Hanoi was first bombed, and she and other children on her street were taken to the mountains, some fifty miles west of Hanoi. They all lived in a large community temple and were cared for by several women who had accompanied them. But they cried for their parents, she recalled, so their guardians decided that the children would be happier if they were divided up and housed with peasant families in the area. The children preferred that because they were with other children, but they also liked learning skills they never had seen in Hanoi: how to plant and harvest rice, how to grow vegetables, and how to tend water buffalo. On some weekends, their parents were able to leave the city and travel by bicycle to visit. It was a long trip, and they had only one night with their children before they returned to Hanoi. If someone's parents did not visit on a particular weekend, the children would cry in sympathy, Phuong recalled, because they thought their friend's parents had been killed in the bombing. Phuong was a Young Pioneer until she was thirteen, and then she was old enough to join the Youth of Ho Chi Minh Communist Association.[30]

Young people such as Nguyen Thi Phuong occupied one end of the age spectrum of Communist women in the North. As they grew older, they occupied a succession of positions: they aided in the fields, made bandages, and helped repair the roads. Soon they, too, were following the three responsibilities. Since the North was a society fighting a total war, all hands were needed. When they were old enough, these women were armed and ready to defend their land.

Most women in rural areas of the North were armed, especially those who lived along the coast, where they were the primary line of defense. They were trained to shoot low, aiming at airplanes that were flying low to bomb the cities. Sometimes they were successful in hitting the aircraft; by their own records, women downed some twenty-eight American bombers. These self-defense and militia units were active with anti-aircraft teams and artillery units, and besides destroying planes, they sunk enemy vessels: one unit succeeded in setting aflame five American vessels, according to the account of several prominent Vietnamese women scholars.[31]

Middle-aged and older women who lived in the cities could perform other tasks. Hoang Thi Chi, eighty-three years old in 1995, was a native of Hanoi. She lost her only son in the war. When her small shop was closed, she cared for and taught neighborhood children. She also served as a nurse, and whenever she and her neighbors heard a plane attacking nearby, they went to the bomb site with a sack of supplies for emergency care. Fortunately, there were no serious bombings near where she lived. There was a bunker in the neighborhood in front of her house so those nearby could hide whenever the air-raid siren blared. After an attack, young people dug out houses and pulled people from the wreckage, while the old provided water, food, and first aid, especially for soldiers who might have to remain in the same position guarding the city all day in case of another attack.[32]

Hoang Thi Chi and other elderly women collected rags for soldiers to use in cleaning their rifles. Their basic tasks were to provide help to the soldiers, to participate in the militia, and to motivate people to evacuate the city when a large bombing raid was expected. Air-raid sirens sounded so often during the bombings of Hanoi that people became indifferent and tended to stay behind instead of going to the shelters. The women ordered them to go, but they themselves remained to tend the wounded and injured. In 1990, Chi was awarded Hero Mother status, since she had lost her son. Although she and her husband had been divorced for many years, his second wife looked after her, and she adopted one of the second wife's sons so she would have a family to take care of her in her old age.[33]

Although the Ho Chi Minh Trail began in the southern part of North Vietnam, ran through Laos, cut through Cambodia, and then entered the South, many women from the North, especially from minority tribes, participated in its building and maintenance. Thousands of women and girls labored on the trail, widening and repairing it and making detours when necessary. They wielded picks and shovels, carrying baskets of dirt and filling holes in the road by day so that trucks could pass at night.[34] Sixteen-year-old Tran Thi Truyen carried a sixty-pound pack and hiked for thirty days down the Ho Chi Minh Trail in the rainy season. She nursed the wounded in a PAVN hospital in southern Laos near the Vietnam border and helped construct an underground surgery unit with a thatched hut on top to sleep in. Although she was shocked by the appalling condition of the casualties, she served the wounded until she was incapacitated by malaria, a common danger on the trail.[35]

The Ho Chi Minh Trail was almost as legendary in North Vietnam as it was in the United States. In 1970, the Vietnam Women's Union published a book of stories that included a few specifically about the trail, while others dealt with women's actions in nearby provinces. The tales were loosely based on fact, but were designed to provide heroic tales for emulation. One narrative, for example, was set in an all-woman's anti-aircraft unit. All the members had lost family members and friends in the American war. When they heard that the Americans were strafing sea-going boats, dropping incendiary and cluster bombs, and distributing psychological propaganda, they became angry and prepared their gun for an attack. They had learned how to take aim, to connect a telephone for communication, and to survey land and spot planes by themselves. When the ships approached, they prepared to attack, and they continued to fire despite heavy opposition. The heroines of the battle were rewarded with membership in the Party. When one girl returned home after the engagement, her mother wept to see her, commenting that now she had become "so skilful [sic] and hardened and could do the job of a boy."[36]

Another story told of a young woman who, by herself, ran a way station for soldiers traveling on the Ho Chi Minh Trail. She provided them with food: rice that was supplied by the army and edible greens that she collected. She also gave them a place to sleep should they need to stop. She always looked for men from her home village, and when she found some, she gave them special treatment in return for a bit of news.[37]

Travel on the trail was critical for the maintenance of Hanoi's war effort, for it ensured that there would be no end to combatants sent to the South. Women rarely traveled south on the trail, unless they were in the army, engaged in nursing duties, or maintaining the trail. Those who worked on the trail lived in nearby villages and were often minority tribespeople. But some who were in need of advanced medical treatment or more education went north following the route. Even more important was that women defended the trail, repaired it, and aided and cared for the male soldiers who traveled its course.

The American bombing campaigns—Rolling Thunder I and II and Linebacker I and II, conducted, respectively, by Presidents Johnson and Nixon—were the most horrifying ordeals for the people of North Vietnam. The Christmas bombing of 1972 and 1973 was the worst. For eleven days, the inhabitants of Hanoi were subject to around-the-clock attacks by American aircraft. The Hanoi government had tried to evacuate nonessential members of the population from the cities since 1966, in anticipation of bombing raids, but many people were reluctant to move to refugee camps, which were overcrowded and full of disease.[38] Although many women and children had evacuated in December 1972, after the breakdown of the Paris peace negotiations, others had not. Some, despite the likelihood of more American bombings, had returned, thinking that the draft treaty negotiated by Henry Kissinger and Le Duc Tho in Paris had meant an end to the war.[39] Despite the evacuation, some 1,300 people were killed in the raids.

Hanoi was surrounded by surface-to-air missiles (SAMs), courtesy of the Soviet Union, and was in fact one of the most heavily defended cities in the world. Additional protection for those who remained in the city was provided by bunkers and individual "spider holes" in the sidewalks, into which passers-by could jump in case of an attack. Some women, like Hoang Thi Chi, remained throughout the bombing to aid the casualties. In February 1994, Pham Thi Vien, president of the Women's Union of Hanoi from 1954 to 1975, told me her story of the Christmas bombing. She was firing a SAM during an air attack on the city when General Vo Nguyen Giap came to tell her that her father had been killed. He asked her if, in her anguish, she could continue to fight. Her response was typically heroic: she said that she would fight on, holding back her tears of mourning in order to see the sky and fire accurately.[40] Afterward, she would grieve for her father.

At the same meeting, Pham Kim Hy described her sorrow at the loss of her son, who in 1994 was still missing in action. She showed me his picture and recited a poem that she had written to his spirit. It spoke of her sorrow over losing him, but her joy that his remains rested in the Truong Son mountains along the Ho Chi Minh Trail, forever part of the fatherland. It is called "The Lullaby":

Your are sleeping deeply on the top of the Truong Son mountain
Do you still hear my lullaby?
The one who has my love and longing
And I always will care for you.

You are sleeping on a grassy field
The lullaby is still being sung by birds instead of me
The one who has my love and longing
My voice is in the country's voice.

You seem so quiet there in the silent Truong Son
Forest flowers still send out perfume.
The one who has my love and longing
And I do your duty for the country.[41]

While there were many heroines in both North and South during the war whose accomplishments are only now being recognized, and countless others whose stories are yet untold, the few women who reached leadership positions indicates something about the relative importance that Vietnamese men granted them. Nguyen Thi Dinh was a self-made leader in battle, and as such was an anomaly in Vietnam, as she would have been (until the 1980s) in the United States. Other women who fought did not go far from their homes, joining guerrilla or self-defense units. Some did outstanding feats of valor worthy of emulation, but the publicity given their acts was meant to stimulate men into fighting—in effect to shame them—and to encourage more women to greater bravery. Women knew their stories through the teaching sessions at the Women's Unions, but often the heroines to be emulated were local, those whom people knew.

A discussion of women's leadership roles has to consider those who did have a worldwide appeal. Since the Hanoi regime considered propaganda a critical part of its attempt to defeat the United States, portraying America as the slayer of women and children was de rigeur, as was using various symbols. Mary Anne Tétreault has described Vietnam's use of women displaying bravery as the "totality of national mobilization, and the extent of sacrifice demanded by the revolution." She also noted the depiction of women on postage stamps, such as that honoring the uprising at Ben Tre. Statues also are powerful symbols, and the one in Hanoi of a woman with a child to mark the spot where a bomb dropped during the Christmas raids of 1972 destroyed a house and killed a family is a powerful memorial to the outrage over the bombing that was felt worldwide.[42] Tétreault argues, though, as have others, that these portrayals of woman as victim or as extraordinary hero are somewhat demeaning, since they do not portray woman as equal. And despite the achievements of the war, it cannot be said that women did win equality.

Only a few women acquired anything like national or international status, although eight were in various leadership ranks of the Provisional Revolutionary Government or the Vietnam Alliance of National, Democratic, and Peace Forces. Madame Nguyen Thi Binh was one of these outstanding women, although it was questionable whether she was a power in her own right or more a symbol. She was the granddaughter of a revolutionary hero in the struggle against the French, Phan Chu Trinh. Born in Saigon, she became a revolutionary as a student in the 1950s and was imprisoned for three years after 1954 for having organized uprisings of students against the French and the Americans who came to aid them. She was a founding member of the National Liberation Front. Binh achieved her greatest fame as the foreign minister of the Provisional Revolutionary Government. She was the representative of the NLF during the long peace talks in Paris. She arrived there in 1968 and served with few breaks until January 1973. The French came to know her so well that she was called by them the "Queen of the Viet Cong,"[43] an indication that they had confused her with Nguyen Thi Dinh, the deputy commander of the PLAF. The Vietnamese did not bother to disabuse them of their misconceptions. Her compatriots honored her for her lineage as well as her activities.

During the war, Binh traveled widely as the representative of the PRG, which the NLF and Hanoi considered to be the legitimate government of South Vietnam. Traveling throughout the Third World, she spoke on behalf of peace and the justice of Vietnam's cause. She helped publicize the NLF and dramatize the inequity of the American war, a powerful nation destroying a weak one, David and Goliath. Although she was one of the best known of the revolutionary women, she kept her private life strictly separate from her public role. During the war, this was perhaps to protect her family, but in the 1990s the reason remains a mystery to the West. The Central Intelligence Agency found that she was married and had two children, but that was all it learned. After the war, she served as minister of education in the Socialist Republic of Vietnam, hence a representative of the entire country. She then became a member of the National Assembly and, from 1994 to 1997, was vice president of Vietnam.

Binh's role in Paris cast her in the public eye like no other Vietnamese woman. She went with the peace delegation representing the NLF, a counterbalance to Le Duc Tho of North Vietnam. Henry Kissinger, who knew her during those years, hated her because he believed that she changed the peace terms and contradicted what Le Duc Tho and he had agreed on. In 1971, she proposed a plan that offered a simple withdrawal of the American forces for a return of prisoners, implying that peace could be settled apart from the question of a provisional government and the issues of Cambodia and Laos. Kissinger called this one of Hanoi's "characteristic duplicitous stunts."[44] In recalling him twenty years later, Nguyen Thi Binh pronounced him "vain."[45]

It has been left to the Vietnam Women's Union to memorialize the heroic actions of the women of the revolution. The war museum in Hanoi had only a few pictures of the long-haired warriors in 1991, and the museum to Ho Chi Minh had none. The women who were most remembered were either those whose exploits symbolized extreme valor, like the woman taking the American pilot captive, or those who had suffered extraordinarily, like the women imprisoned in Cu Chi.

The women of the North occupied a very different position in the revolution than did those of the South. They were part of a total war, their duties carefully outlined in the statement of the three responsibilities. Occasionally, at meetings such as the May 8 commemoration of International Women's Day, emulation stories would be told of their exceptional bravery or ability to withstand physical hardship, to fill men's shoes, and to endure life under heavy bombing. But there were no prison camps in the North comparable to Con Dao, and northern women did not live among the enemy, as the women of the NLF did. Hence they were not subject to torture, and few women, even those who achieved military distinction in the PAVN, were known outside the North. However, they were an indispensable part of the war, freeing men to carry the conflict south, defending their own villages, and raising children who could perpetuate the conflict to the next generation.

7

. . . .
AFTER THE SHOOTING STOPPED

April 30, 1975, brought an end to the long struggle. In the South, NLF supporters, women as well as men, celebrated the event that the North called liberation, and the losers accepted the new order or attempted to flee the country. In retrospect, the role that the long-haired warriors—women in both South and North who supported the Communist cause—played in the conflict is both easy and hard to assess. One measure of evaluating women's significance is to compare the women of the NLF and the Hanoi regime with the supporters of the Saigon government.

In the North, members of the Women's Union, and the Women's Liberation Association in the South affiliated with the NLF, were an asset to their cause. They supported the men, providing them with the food they ate, the uniforms or clothing they wore, the hammocks they slept in, even the primitive medicines they carried. Some fought with them along the Ho Chi Minh Trail or in the jungles of the central highlands or the Mekong Delta. Others, in the North, constituted the home guard, served as air-raid wardens in the cities under attack, and provided intelligence. They watched the skies for enemy aircraft, sounded the alarm, urged people to evacuate, and cared for the casualties. If their husbands or sons went south, they encouraged them, even sending a second child to war when one son was killed. If the men did not return, they accepted their losses, even if they were deprived by government policy of learning their loved ones' fate. They grieved for their losses, as all wives and mothers would, but they did not mount anti-war protests or attempt to influence the government to stop the war. They believed, as Ho Chi Minh said, that they might have to fight a hundred or a thousand years to win independence, but there was no alternative.

The revolutionary women cultivated the crops, freeing men to fight, and they learned to be not only farmers, but also doctors, nurses, teachers, spies, propagandists, and entertainers. They raised their children and did their best to save them from injury or death. They were loyal to the cause and accepted the sacrifices it entailed because they were convinced that independence demanded it. Many were sincere believers in Communist doctrine and thought that with peace they would be able to live in a society based on its tenets. Others just hoped that an end to war would bring lasting peace.

The women of the NLF were also committed, if in a different way. They often knew little of Communist ideology, but they had experienced oppression on a personal level. They had hated the French and came to loath the Americans because they were foreigners, outsiders, who sought to impose an alien belief system and culture on them. The French had brought the inequities of racism and colonialism, while the Americans delivered the horrors of high-tech warfare, which subjected them to more bombardment than all areas of conflict had suffered during World War II. In addition, the guerrillas of the NLF and their families lived with the burdens of chemical defoliation, lack of food, malnutrition, little or no medical care, torture, and often imprisonment and death. Some did indeed venerate Ho Chi Minh, while for others fear of bombing, revenge for the deaths of those they loved, and hatred of the corrupt, venal, and American-sponsored Saigon government and its military establishment was enough. For all these reasons and more, the NLF women learned to fight, to spy, and to support the Communist cause.

One might speculate that women whose husbands or sons fought for the ARVN could become a burden to their government. Their spouses feared leaving them where they might be molested by foreign or Saigon troops. In defoliated areas, they suffered from lack of food, since their fields and crops were destroyed. Made refugees, they had no homes and no work; their children were malnourished and often ill. If the Communist enemy came, there was no one to defend them, and they could be ravished by those troops as well. By the end of the war, many of the women, especially those who were widowed or unmarried, had become prostitutes or bar girls to support themselves and their children.

Many peasants in areas controlled by the Saigon government lived in fear for their lives. They could be killed by the NLF, the Americans, even the Saigon troops—random casualties, caught in the crossfire. They did not fight and tried to escape the firefights, but they were everywhere. When the peasants became refugees, they added to their government's problems—neither enemy nor friend, simply pawns that had to be moved, housed, fed, or left to die.

Fear for the safety of their families could cause ARVN soldiers to flee the battlefield. By the early spring of 1975, when the tide of battle turned decisively against the army of President Nguyen Van Thieu, the ARVN retreated to save their women and families, some of whom were with them, while others returned to Saigon. The retreat became a rout, and the PAVN and PLAF were successful. They—and their women—had won the war. Women could be either assets or liabilities in wartime, and in the Communist victory they may well have been a benefit to the forces of the revolution.

When victory came, women who had participated in the long war reacted in different ways to its aftermath. Nguyen Thi Dinh, a leader of the NLF forces, took up offices in the building in Saigon that had once housed General William Westmoreland. She worked with the Vietnam Women's Union and some years later became its president and moved to Hanoi. Her son, who had spent the war in the North, was dead. Nguyen Thi Binh returned to Hanoi in January 1973, before the completion of negotiations of the Paris Peace Accords, which resulted in the American withdrawal. While Le Duc Tho and Henry Kissinger were named *Time*'s men of the year in 1972 (Tho declined the honor), she was not mentioned. After serving in the cabinet and legislature, she continued her travels as spokesperson for the women of her country. In 1992 she became vice president of the country, a relatively powerless position; she retired in 1997. Duong Quynh Hoa served the liberated state for a few months in the cabinet of the Provisional Revolutionary Government of the NLF, but she resigned her membership in the Party and commuted between her villa in Saigon—renamed Ho Chi Minh City— and Paris. The new regime did not live up to her expectations; it was unscrupulous and avaricious, and did not reflect the idealism that she had anticipated. As she told journalist Stanley Karnow in 1981, the thousands of Northerners who had moved south to fill in the ranks after the decimation of the NLF during the Tet Offensive behaved in a rigid, doctrinaire manner, which she loathed. He recalled her saying, "They behave as if they had conquered us."[1] Victory did not erase that feeling for many former members of the NLF. In 1976, it was intensified when the North did indeed incorporate the South into a united Vietnam ruled from Hanoi by Northerners.

Other women besides Duong Quynh Hoa found the new regime lacking, but some did very well. Madame Nguyen Thi Thi, a former guerrilla, was head of a food-processing monopoly. According to Karnow, she "streamlined its bureaucracy, insisted on profits and expanded the firm to include eighteen factories, eight hundred retail outlets and some seven thousand employees." The monopoly exported millions of dollars of goods. Having mastered that challenge, Madame Thi focused her talents on other projects. By the end of the 1980s, she was directing an offshore-oil project and a rice-marketing network. She told an interviewer that the nation needed fewer cadres and more accountants.[2] Nguyen Thi Rao also excelled at business, going into food processing.

Although several years passed before a few women were elected to the National Assembly, some prominent women served in Vietnam's mission to the United Nations.

Other well-known women had mixed feelings about the outcome of the war. Madame Nguyen Phuoc Dai, who had been educated in Paris and had an outstanding law practice in Saigon, was forced to close her office; she turned it into a restaurant, La Bibliothèque, which foreign journalists came to enjoy, as much for her excellent food as for her spicy gossip and complaints. Madame Ngo Ba Thanh, who had worked with a group of intellectuals for peace and had been beaten and tortured by the Saigon regime for her efforts, remained in Vietnam, but she traveled internationally, continuing her search for justice.

Countless other women shared the immediate joy that came with the end of the conflict: soldiers returned home, and the prisons were liberated—the guards killed and the prisoners released. The branches of the Women's Union prepared to instruct women in the arts of peace instead of war: basic literacy, health education, good nutrition, child care. The women who had served as prostitutes during the war were taken for rehabilitation, in hopes the new state could avoid the evils of the old. But a shortage of jobs and lack of skills left many of them bereft.

Yet the lives of the people did not improve as they had hoped. The devastation of the war—the thousands of deaths, the maimed and injured, the thousands of missing in action, the thousands of refugees, problems of malnutrition and disease—continued to plague the people. The land suffered from bomb craters, defoliation, chemical poisoning, and destruction of the topsoil by bombs, rain, and deliberate actions of American weapons to prevent its use to raise crops for the NLF. Land mines and unexploded ordnance were lethal for peasant farmers and unwary children. In addition, the country lacked schools, universities, hospitals, houses, roads, bridges, railroads, airports, and seaports. Rebuilding them proved an overwhelming expense for the new regime to manage. Aid from the Soviet Union was not enough to counterbalance the trade embargo imposed by the United States, and when in 1976 Hanoi incorporated the South into its rigid economic structure, the whole country suffered. Refugees had been fleeing the country since the end of the war, but in 1976, with reunification, many Chinese, their businesses in the South confiscated, fled the country, part of the first wave of boat people. The war with Pol Pot's Cambodia (renamed Democratic Kampuchea), fought between 1977 and 1979, added to the country's miseries, as did the subsequent decade-long occupation of Kampuchea. The fleeing "boat people," who trusted their lives to flimsy boats on the high seas, taking the chance that they would be rescued by humanitarian seamen rather than suffering robbery, rape, and death at the hands of pirates, shocked the rest of the world. While those who survived the perils of the sea eventually found new homes in many countries—Canada, the United States, France, Australia—the rest of the world boycotted trade with Vietnam, since it had violated the United Nations Charter by invading its ruthless neighbor. Vietnam's people suffered for the foreign policies of its government, and only the Soviet Union and a few other neutral or socialist nations came to its aid. As usual, women, the old, and children suffered disproportionately in times of hardship. Inadequate health services did not prevent the country's population from ballooning; by the end of the 1980s, it was over 70 million. Barely surviving in the best of times, the peasants were submerged in times of drought, typhoon, flood, and crop failure. The country, once part of the giant "rice bowl" of Southeast Asia, did not become self-sufficient in rice until the early 1990s, and it was still one of the poorest countries in the world.

In the most basic ways, the lot of the Vietnamese woman did not change. She was mother and wife and worked in the rice paddies or office or factory. Since she was poorly educated, if at all, her children also lacked quality education. Le Thi, director of the Center for Women's Research in Ho Chi

Minh City, noted that in the North, it was the wife who bore the largest share of work. She also did the majority of agricultural work and all the domestic chores. Yet men were the decision makers and determined major issues regarding the family, including how many children they should have, and whether the wife should be allowed to use birth control. As usual, the woman was held to a standard of absolute fidelity, while the man could do as he pleased. Le Thi also noted that cases of men abusing their women and children was common. Wives were also oppressed by their mothers-in-law and had to accept their husbands taking a concubine if they could not bear children. In other words, little had changed from the past, and happiness for women and children was as far from reality as ever.[3]

Thus it is easy to conclude that Vietnamese women did not gain equality with men in any meaningful way. The military museum built in Hanoi to honor the history of Vietnam's wars made scarcely a mention of their contributions. A few striking photographs of marching long-haired warriors were the single example of their achievements. In 1995, the Women's Union in Hanoi looked like any other drab building that needed a coat of paint, and the activities behind its walls, and in the many smaller offices around the city and countryside, were notable more for what they lacked—books, paper and pencils, office equipment, and, in the countryside, medicines and student's books—than for what they showed. In Ho Chi Minh City, the women themselves raised the money for a museum honoring their efforts, and they had to locate artifacts from the war to fill its display cases.

What had happened? Were the promises of a new society in vain? Or was it simply that in the devastation, poverty, and isolation during the decades after the war everyone had to suffer, there was minimal aid from outside, and social experimentation was more punitive than humanitarian. The "New Economic Zones" into which the urban refugees were resettled were in harsh, inhospitable land, and those who were relocated had few tools or skills with which to farm. The country remained overwhelmingly peasant, and its agricultural techniques were primitive. When the Communist government collectivized the land, the peasants responded by slowing production and cutting output. Women returned to their traditional roles of wives and mothers and took up their hoes and rakes. Their most urgent needs were for food and medications so they could care for their children, but Western medicines were in short supply and too expensive. Eastern medicines would have to suffice. The Women's Union tried to solve these problems, but it could not compensate for the dearth of supplies. The American government would not allow nongovernmental organizations to ship medical supplies to Vietnam until the early 1980s, and there was a ban on everything else due to the trade embargo imposed at the end of the war with the United States.

The women who had participated in the war remembered their sacrifices. History seemed to have forgotten them, even in their own land, but they could remember through storytelling, and they did. When it appeared that their stories would be totally lost, they determined to remember them through the creation of museums to preserve and exhibit their photographs and artifacts. These museums were not open every day or for many hours, nor were they on the main tourist circuits that began to appear in the mid-1990s. They are not the equivalent of museums honoring the country's (male) history, but they are a start.[4]

One place where women's history abounds is on the prison island of Con Dao, the former French prison of Poulo Condore. In early 1994, I sailed to the island with a group of Vietnamese women and men who had been imprisoned there during the war. They brought their children to show them what the infamous prison, abandoned since April 30, 1975, looked like, and to teach them of its history. They told their stories to me and my American companions, and they and a local guide showed us around the historic part of the island. The buildings were almost intact, since the tropical weather could do little to destroy structures made of large stone blocks and iron bars. The cell blocks stretched in parallel lines, with enclosures open for entrance and exit, across from the infamous tiger cages. In a small museum was displayed the record book the French had kept, listing the prisoners, the dates of their confinements, and, in many cases, the dates of their executions.

Con Dao is lush and green, with picturesque white sand beaches and a few very small fishing villages. The fishermen go to sea in sampans whose prows are decorated with eyes, to watch for evil spirits in the ocean. When we sailed there, the South China Sea was calm and tranquil, but it can be violent when a typhoon strikes. Even in the best of weather, the voyage from Vung Tao takes sixteen hours; escape from the island would have been impossible.

The prison was built in 1862, just a year after the French conquered Saigon. Its stone walls were cold in the wet season, when the monsoon rains drenched the land, and hot in the dry season. Little air penetrated the cells. In French times, the prisoners had been worked, sometimes to death, and that practice continued under the administration of the Saigon regime. A road that the French had attempted to construct over the mountains separating one side of the island from the other lay in ruins in 1994; no matter how many men's lives were sacrificed to the construction project, the jungle finally won. By the time of the American war, the prison was the largest in the extensive system the South Vietnamese and their American advisers constructed: it held some 10,000 inmates. Some were there for minor infractions; others, for crimes deemed major—terrorist activities, assassinations, intelligence gathering, arms smuggling. But whatever the crime, the inmates suffered conditions so bad that they were converted to Communism, regardless of their political beliefs when they were admitted. The administrators wanted to confine their political opponents, to extract information from them, to break their spirits, or to let the harsh conditions destroy them if they did not die from torture, illness, or malnutrition.[5]

The women with us had dressed for the occasion. All wore beautiful *ao dais,* nothing like what they had been clothed in during their imprisonment. Their outfits and the way they had dressed their children seemed to demonstrate the importance they attached to being on the island; it was their first visit since their incarceration, and they probably would not return. The women told stories of pain and misery. Thieu Thi Tam and her sister, Tao, had been imprisoned on Con Dao when they were teenagers. At fifteen, Tam had been the youngest prisoner. The sisters had been held in a large compound with an open pit for defecation; the pit still stank, twenty years later. Tam, who had a lovely voice, sang for us, in memory of Vo Thi Sau, a sixteen-year-old girl taken prisoner and executed by the French. She had shot a French soldier, but today is regarded as a heroine; streets are named after her in many cities of the South, just as they are for Nguyen Thi Minh Khai, who was guillotined in 1941 and is celebrated as a heroine throughout the country.

Another woman, Nguyen Thi Thuc, had been a liberation commando during the long war; she still held fast to its principles and was an important Party official. She had been imprisoned in the cells for which Con Dao was infamous: the five- by eight-foot tiger cages, in which five or eight women were shackled together. Thuc had been a prisoner in 1970 when the humanitarian worker Donald Luce visited the prison with Representative Augustus

Hawkins and his aide Tom Harkins. Luce, who knew Vietnamese, had heard of the top-secret prison and overheard from the guards that women were confined there. He demanded to see them and found them only when the women screamed to get his attention. The entryway was hidden at the end of a long corridor with a small door at the end; a pile of wood concealed it from passers-by, and the guard showing them around steadfastly denied that it was there.[6]

Nguyen Thi Thuc showed the prison to her young daughter, who gave it the attention any child of ten might give a place where events had happened long before she was born. The place had more significance to the former prisoners; the women looked for graves of women they had known and located one another's cells. The large monument to Vo Thi Sau, whose grave (or some one else's chosen at random to represent it) was decorated with elaborate stonework and fresh flowers, testified to her willingness to sacrifice. Even the young, female and male, had died for their country.

As we sailed away from Con Dao, Nguyen Thi Thuc stood at the stern of the ship, staring back at the island, the lovely beach, and the terrible prison. No one disturbed her as she lost herself in her memories. She had been a prisoner from 1970 to 1975. She was there when news came of the defeat of the Saigon regime, and she joined her comrades in the uprising on May 1 that resulted in their freedom.[7]

Every war has its victims, its heros, its casualties, and its memories. The Vietnam conflict, like many wars in the twentieth century, forced many of the losers into exile. Among those who stayed in Vietnam, not all found that the creation of the Socialist Republic of Vietnam in 1976 brought the paradise of which they had dreamed. Some, like Truong Nhu Tang, who had spent his life fighting for the National Liberation Front, learned rather soon that victory in the South meant rule by the North.[8] Others defected more recently, the book by Bui Tin, *Following Ho Chi Minh*, is even more striking considering his rank in the North Vietnamese Army and his importance as a journalist.[9] Others in the South who were associated at a very low level with the Americans could not help but remain bitter.

Those who were closely associated with the old regime or the Americans often were incarcerated in reeducation camps, where they were taught to think like the winners and made to suffer by manual labor and harsh conditions for having chosen the wrong side. For some, this imprisonment led to death by overwork, malnutrition, and disease; for others, ultimate release and flight from their homeland.

For others, whose roles were less important, the first decade of Communist rule was difficult. Luong Thi Kim Vinh had served as a translator for the Americans, particularly those who worked for the Rand Corporation interviewing defectors and captives. When the war ended, the rest of her family fled the country, but she was never successful. The new regime distrusted her, so work was hard to obtain, and her skill in English was of no use when Russian was the most prized foreign language. After eleven years, as the United States and Vietnam edged slowly closer to each other, Kim Vinh found that her language abilities were useful. She taught English and eventually became the associate dean of the Faculty of Foreign Languages at the Open University in Ho Chi Minh City, a private institution where workers and older students who could afford to pay minimal fees could study to improve their chances for better employment. English would serve them in good stead as they prepared for the return of Americans and other foreigners in an open economy that welcomed businesspeople and tourists. Kim Vinh, who had long before abandoned notions of leaving her country, could easily serve the new regime.[10]

For those on the winning side who liked what they saw and tolerated the harshness of life after victory, socialism brought some rewards. The foreigners were gone; the war was over. If poverty overwhelmed the land, at best all suffered together. They had to rebuild after thirty years of war and to recover from losses that virtually every family suffered. Soon memorials began to appear: instead of cemeteries for the ARVN dead, which were destroyed, monuments capped the many graveyards of the PAVN and the NLF. Veterans were not hard to spot, either, since their prosthetics were crude and homemade; however, since two wars were fought after that with the United States, it was not possible to determine the conflict that had caused the casualty. For veterans who could get about, attempts to find any kind of work were essential. For those who could not take care of themselves, there were rest homes, tucked away from prying eyes. Women were housed there as well as men—those who had lost limbs. Those who had lost their minds, and there were some, were kept out of sight by family or government.

The long-haired warriors had their reunions, as did the men. By the late 1980s, when a semblance of prosperity returned following the adoption of *doi moi*, or a market economy, women who had fought together gathered to reminisce. The pilgrimage to Con Dao, such as we had participated in, was only one of many. The Vietnam Women's Union encourages such gatherings, for it knows that as the elder generation dies, their stories disappear. Only by tending their memories will the women warriors retain their place in the history of their country.

It is not appropriate to end a work on Vietnam's women by focusing on pain, suffering, and the lack of achievement. The magazine *Women of Vietnam* presents a far more optimistic account. Openly and proudly Communist, its authors take pride in their memories of Uncle Ho: they celebrated the 107th anniversary of his birth in May 1997 at the Eighth Congress of the Vietnam Women's Union. In preparation for that congress, they agreed to emphasize five issues:

- Increasing women's knowledge;
- Creating jobs for women at salary levels equal to that of men;
- Improvement of health care for women and children, including education in family planning and efforts to prevent social ills;
- Involvement in the making of laws and social policies that have a direct bearing on the welfare of women and children; and
- Developing and strengthening the administration of the Women's Union by inviting more young intellectuals to participate.

The Women's Union also emphasized its participation in the plan of action adopted at the Beijing Women's Conference held in 1995, which included immunizing children, fighting to reduce the worldwide incidence of AIDS and STDs, and preventing the trafficking of women and children in Laos and Cambodia.[11]

Work for the benefit of women in rural areas also was stressed. In 1993 the union, together with UNICEF, began a program to ensure the availability of clean water and hygienic latrines. The union also has enabled rural women to receive training in new technologies, participate in self-help programs, and borrow funds to create employment opportunities that will help to raise their standard of living.[12]

Urban intellectual women are, in the mid-1990s, concentrating on research and teaching designed to raise the level of women. Bui Thi Kim Quy, a sociologist at Ho Chi Minh City University, established the first women's studies program there in 1991, charting new fields of study in work on women. Interaction among Vietnamese intellectuals, American scholars, and women active in international women's movements brings new information and help for the women of Vietnam. Where questions by foreign women visiting Vietnam about its women were once met with silence, now at meetings women are present who can answer them and engage in dialogue on common issues.

Yet the peasant women of the National Liberation Front, especially those who were uneducated and unskilled, remain in the background. Women like Vo Thi Thang, the attractive smiling sapper who went to prison despite the efforts of attorney Ngo Ba Thanh to save her from Con Dao, are visible, but most are not. Their wartime careers surprise the women who know them. Nguyen Thi Minh Hang, a Catholic intellectual who with her husband teaches English in Ho Chi Minh City, was greatly surprised to discover that her elderly cook was a former Viet Cong. Even Nguyen Thi Phuong, who grew up in the North and participated in the war, was surprised to learn that her housekeeper in Saigon was a former revolutionary. The villagers of Dinh Thuy and countless others like them live on meager rations because the government cannot afford to reward them for their heroic sacrifices.[13]

Even those who are themselves well off recognize that their sisters have suffered unequally as a result of the war. The peasant women from the Mekong Delta who come to Dr. Nguyen Thi Ngoc Phuong at the Tu Du Hospital for Mothers and Infants in Ho Chi Minh City with problem pregnancies demonstrate the persistence of the war's ills on future generations. The disproportionate number of malformed and aborted fetuses kept in formaldehyde-filled jars in storage there has a message for the visitor allowed to see them. Scholar Katheleen Barry wrote: "The enduring costs to women of war may well be the greatest untold story of war."[14] For many women, poverty, not honor, is the legacy of the war. Their own government has yet to acknowledge that price.

The Vietnam Women's Union did not forget the past. It called for "upholding [women's] glorious tradition of 'heroism, undauntedness, loyalty and resourcefulness' in the past resistance against foreign aggression for national salvation and on the strength of their self-help spirit." And in a picture of women in colorful minority dress was Vo Thi Thang, the woman of the persistent smile who had participated in the sapper attack on Brink's Hotel in Saigon in 1964 and had been sent to Con Dao. She is still beautiful—and still smiling.[15]

NOTES

• • • • • • • • • • • • • • •

Introduction

1. Dieu-Hong is a pseudonym. Most names in this text are accurate, so far as the author knows. But during the war, aliases were common, and some women appear to have retained them. I have used Vietnamese name order, by which the family name precedes the middle name and then the given name. Vietnamese go by their given name, which may change throughout their lifetime—nicknames for children, pseudonyms during war, and the like. Vietnamese is a monosyllabic language. The name of the country, Vietnam, is Western usage; in Vietnam, it is written as two words: Viet Nam. The Americans condensed it, as they did the name of Hanoi (Ha Noi), Saigon (Sai Gon), Danang (Da Nang), Dalat (Da Lat), and many other cities and towns to suit their preferences. Lately, the site of the famous battle, Dien Bien Phu, has become one word, as have Viet Minh and even Viet Cong, now fallen into disuse. One might argue that I am arbitrary in my preferences, and I plead guilty.

2. Jeffrey Race, *War Comes to Long An* (Berkeley: University of California Press, 1972); Lady Borton, *After Sorrow: An American Among the Vietnamese* (New York: Viking, 1995), book 1, 3–132. Borton's book relies heavily on her twenty-five years of living and working as a Quaker in Vietnam. I am deeply indebted to her inspiration and wisdom.

3. One of Borton's friends in Ban Long village expressed amazement that the Americans fought with a ratio of one fighting man in battle and nine behind the lines, providing support. The Vietnamese had no support other than what they

themselves provided, and they, the women, were the fighters. See Borton, *After Sorrow,* 73.

4. Professor Bui Thi Kim Quy, Institute of Social Sciences, interview with author, Ho Chi Minh City, 8 November 1995; Borton, *After Sorrow,* 37.

5. The Tu Du gynecological hospital in Ho Chi Minh City, headed by Dr. Nguyen Thi Ngoc Phuong and her staff of several hundred, cared for these women. The physicians found an exceptionally large number of tumors and cancers of the ovaries, uterus, and cervix. They also delivered and separated Siamese twins, who lived at the hospital when their parents rejected them as defective. The herbicides continued to affect people in the South, as determined by measuring and comparing the level of dioxin in the tissues of people from North and South. Stillbirths remain a problem: many aborted deformed fetuses remain in the hospital, preserved in large jars of formaldehyde on shelves in a back room. I visited the hospital first with John McAuliff and the U.S.–Indochina Reconciliation Project study tour in January 1986. On my third trip, in mid-September 1992, I went there again, with a group of students and faculty from the University of Utah. The hospital was founded by money from the East German government and was well maintained, although equipment and medicine was, in 1995, still in short supply. Scientific evidence that dioxin was the sole cause of the tragedy is controversial, and Phuong herself carefully avoids making that conclusion.

6. Nguyen Thi Dinh, "No Other Road to Take" recorded by Tran Huong Nam, translated by Mai Van Elliott, Data Paper 102 (Southeast Asia Program, Cornell University, 1976).

7. Borton, *After Sorrow,* 109. Borton described how, even in the small delta village where she lived and worked, there had been an increase in crime and greed as a result of *doi moi.*

8. Hoang Ngoc Nguyen of Ho Chi Minh City, whom I interviewed in Salt Lake City on 15 May 1995, told me that the government was now paying women over seventy years old $20 a month for their wartime service. That payment had just begun.

9. Stories of the individual women appear throughout the text.

10. Mary Ann Tétreault, "Vietnam," in *Women and Revolution in Africa, Asia, and the New World,* edited by Mary Ann Tétreault (Columbia: University of South Carolina Press, 1994), 122–23.

1. Revolutionary Women

1. George C. Herring, *America's Longest War,* 3rd ed. (New York: Wiley, 1996).

2. In Vietnamese, the three responsibilities are cited in *Tu Dieh Viet-Anh* (Vietnamese–English Dictionary) (Ho Chi Minh City: Ho Chi Minh, 1997). I thank Huynh Quang Thanh of Ho Chi Minh City, now in Salt Lake City, for his translation.

3. Ut Tich's life was recounted in one of the best known novels about the war: Nguyen Thi, *Nguoi Me Cam Sung* (The Mother Who Holds a Gun) (Hanoi: Litera-

ture and Arts, 1965). I am indebted to Hoang Ngoc Nguyen, of Salt Lake City, for bringing this to my attention.

4. At this point, she added her husband's name to hers, becoming Ut Tich. Information from Huynh Quang Tranh.

5. "South Vietnamese Guerrillas of the Present Resistance," *Some Aspects of Guerilla [sic] Warfare in Vietnam* (probably Hanoi: Foreign Language Press, 1965), Pike Collection, Texas Tech University, Lubbock, Unit 5, 1965. Since the collection was being reorganized as I was researching, I have not included box or file number. Ut Tich is also mentioned in "PLAF Representative's Report at E. Nam Bo PLAF Congress," Liberation Radio broadcast to South Vietnam, in Vietnamese, 19 October 71, Pike Collection, NLF, Unit 5, 1971. Ut Tich tells her own story in *Heroes and Heroines of the Liberation Armed Forces of South Vietnam* (Saigon: Liberation Editions, 1965), Pike Collection, 1965.

6. *Guong Sang Soi Chung: Ban Thanh Tich Cac Nu Chien Si* (Brilliant Examples to Emulate: The Distinguished Services of Women-Fighters) (Saigon: Women's Liberation Association, 1965, 1966), Pike Collection, 1966–1967. The reprint edition, signed by Nguyen Huu Tho, chairman of the NLF, bestowed the Bulwark Medal First Class on all women of South Vietnam (presumably all female guerrillas.) The document was captured in Binh Duong Province, November 1966. Ut Tich's life was fictionally recounted in *Nguoi Me Cam Sung,* and a brief version appears in TranVan Giau, ed., *Truyen Thong Cach Mang Cua Phu Nu Nam Bo Thanh Dong* (The Revolutionary Tradition of Women in Southern Vietnam) (Ho Chi Minh City: Vietnam Women's Union, 1989), 536. My thanks to Hoang Ngoc Nguyen and Huynh Quang Thanh for their assistance on the information.

7. Douglas Pike, *Viet Cong: The Organization and Techniques of the National Liberation Front of South Vietnam* (Cambridge, Mass.: MIT Press, 1966), 172–77.

8. Ho used countless aliases in his life, from the time he left Vietnam in 1911 to his return in 1941. His birth name was perhaps Nguyen That Thanh, his name as a Comintern member was probably Nguyen Ai Quoc, and the name by which history knows him is Ho Chi Minh.

9. The Communists were not the first group to fight for women's rights. The literary group Tu Luc Van Doan (Self-Reliance Literary Club) was the first organized effort to aid them. But under the French regime, little could happen aside from talk, and that under very guarded circumstances.

10. Nguyen Khac Vien, "A Century of National Struggle: The August Revolution," *Vietnamese Studies,* no. 24 (1947): 136–38.

11. My notes of 10 February 1994, taken at the Vietnam Women's Union in Hanoi, indicate the women's belief that he had said that, although his written texts do not reveal such specificity.

12. Nguyen Khac Vien, "A Century of National Struggle," 136–38.

13. Ho Chi Minh, "Appeal Made on the Occasion of the Founding of the Communist Party of Indochina," February 18, 1930, in *Ho Chi Minh on Revolution: Selected Writings, 1920–66,* edited by Bernard B. Fall (Boulder, Colo.: Westview, 1984), 129.

14. Pike, *Viet Cong,* 80. Pike argues that the conditions in the South were such as to justify the use of the term "insurgency," rather than "revolution," for the opposition.

15. According to Pham Tam, a Vietnamese Buddhist who fled the country during the Thieu–Ky regime (1965–1975), there were five big prisons in the south: Tan Hiep; Chi Hoa; Thu Duc, which was for women; Phu Quoc, on an island near Cambodia; and Con Dao, considered the worst of all. In addition, there were fifty-eight prisons in each of the fifty-eight provinces. See Pham Tam, *Imprisonment and Torture in South Vietnam* (Maisons Alfort: Fellowship of Reconciliation for the Overseas Vietnamese Buddhist Association, n.d.).

16. Luong Thi Trang, interview with author, Ben Tre, 9 November 1995, translated by Nguyen Thi Sau.

17. Luong Thi Trang, interview with author, Ben Tre, 9 November 1995, translated by Nguyen Thi Sau.

18. Neil L. Jamieson, *Understanding Vietnam* (Berkeley: University of California Press, 1993), 108. Poetry had traditionally been part of the culture of the elite, but in the 1920s and 1930s it was incorporated into popular culture.

19. Nguyen Khac Vien, ed., "Political Program of the National Front for Liberation," *Vietnamese Studies,* no. 18–19, (1967): 362–63.

20. Political goals and ideology shaped the memory of past events. See Linda J. Yarr, "Gender and the Allocation of Time: Impact on the Household Economy," in *Vietnam's Women in Transition,* edited by Kathleen Barry (New York: St. Martin's Press, 1996), 112–13. Some of Communism's promises were written into the first constitution of the Democratic Republic of Vietnam in 1945. See Mary Ann Tétreault, "Vietnam," in *Women and Revolution in Africa, Asia, and the New World,* edited by Mary Ann Tétreault (Columbia: University of South Carolina Press, 1994), 114–15.

21. Daphne Patai, "U.S. Academics and Third World Women: Is Ethical Research Possible?" in *Women's Words: The Feminist Practice of Oral History,* edited by Sherna Berger Gluck and Daphne Patai (New York: Routledge, 1991), 137–41.

22. On the general subject, see Robert E. McGlone, "Rescripting a Troubled Past: John Brown's Family and the Harpers Ferry Conspiracy," *Journal of American History* 75 (1989): 1179–82.

23. Ibid., 1182.

24. David Thelen, "Memory and American History," *Journal of American History* 75 (1989): 1118–20. In the controversy at the Smithsonian Institution in 1995 over the display of the bomber *Enola Gay* and the discussion of the need to drop the atomic bombs on Japan to end World War II, one sees much the same issue in an American context. To dispute an article of faith to many veterans seemed heresy, and, in the end, the airplane and the offending captions were not displayed.

25. Cynthia Enloe, "Women After Wars: Puzzles and Warnings," in *Vietnam's Women in Transition,* edited by Barry, pp. 299–315. Many of the women at the Women's Unions that I visited expressed this fear to me, and they urged me to write their stories, for themselves as much as for anyone else. In Ho Chi Minh City, the

Women's Union collected money from the city's women and coerced them into turning over artifacts so that the historical record could be preserved. Nguyen Thi Lien, interview with author, Ho Chi Minh City, 8 November 1995, translated by Nguyen Thi Sau.

26. Jamieson, *Understanding Vietnam*, 8.

27. Mai Thi Tu and Le Thi Nham Tuyet, *Women in Viet Nam* (Hanoi: Foreign Languages, 1978), 27–29.

28. Ibid., 34; David G. Marr, *Vietnamese Tradition on Trial, 1920–1945* (Berkeley: University of California Press, 1982), 194–99; Nguyen Khac Vien, *Vietnam: A Long History* (Hanoi: Foreign Languages, 1987), 9, 14–15.

29. Barbara Cohen, *The Vietnam Guidebook* (New York: Harper & Row, 1990), 42.

30. Mai and Le, *Women in Viet Nam*, 41–43.

31. Marr, *Vietnamese Tradition on Trial*, 193.

32. My thanks to Hoang Ngoc Nguyen for this information.

33. Jamieson, *Understanding Vietnam*, 27.

34. Tétreault, "Vietnam," 112.

35. Mai and Le, *Women in Viet Nam*, 92.

36. Numerous examples of mistreatment are cited in Tran Tu Binh, *The Red Earth: A Vietnamese Memoir of Life on a Colonial Rubber Plantation*, Monographs in International Studies, Southeast Asia Series, no. 66, translated by John Spragens, Jr., edited by David G. Marr (Athens: Ohio University, 1985), esp. 27.

37. Tétreault, "Vietnam," 112, citing Mai and Le, *Women in Viet Nam*, 30–31.

38. Hue-Tam Ho Tai, *Radicalism and the Origins of the Vietnamese Revolution* (Cambridge, Mass.: Harvard University Press, 1992), 89–113; Marr, *Vietnamese Tradition on Trial*, 190–251.

39. Tai, *Radicalism*, 198–201.

40. Mai and Le, *Women in Viet Nam*, 94–95. Polygamy was legalized under the Gia Long Code, and then the Annam Civil Code, both enacted under the Nguyen Dynasty and continued by the French.

41. Tétreault, "Vietnam," 114. She states that this familiar saying has a variety of phrasing, as does another popular statement: "When the enemy comes, even women have to fight."

42. In recent years, as documents from the former Soviet Union have become available, more proof exists that Ho, or Nguyen Ai Quoc, was married at least once, perhaps having one wife in Moscow and another in China.

43. Mai and Le, *Women in Viet Nam*, 116–17.

44. Members of Vietnam Women's Union, interviews with author, Hanoi, 4 February 1994, translated by Hoang Cong Thuy.

45. William J. Duiker, *Sacred War: Nationalism and Revolution in a Divided Vietnam* (New York: McGraw-Hill, 1995), 39–42.

46. Marc S. Gallicchio, *The Cold War Begins in Asia: American East Asian Policy and the Fall of the Japanese Empire* (New York: Columbia University Press, 1988), 106. The OSS episode is recounted in Stanley Karnow, *Vietnam: A History* (1983;

. . . .

reprint, New York: Penguin, 1991), 148–51. See also Archimedes L. A. Patti, *Why Viet Nam? Prelude to America's Albatross* (Berkeley: University of California Press, 1980.) The complex year of 1945, which had such devastating consequences in Southeast Asia and around the globe as World War II came to an end, has been studied in an important work by David G. Marr, *Vietnam 1945: The Quest for Power* (Berkeley: University of California Press, 1995).

47. One such woman was Duong Quynh Hoa, from a wealthy Chinese family in Saigon. She studied medicine in Paris, and she and her sister became adherents of Communism there from their contacts with Ho Chi Minh and other radicals. Her story is recounted extensively in the text.

48. Mai and Le, *Women in Viet Nam,* 129.

49. Marr, *Vietnamese Tradition on Trial,* 244–45, citing Ton The Que, *Chi Mot Con Duong,* 95.

50. David G. Marr, *Vietnamese Tradition on Trial,* 246–47, citing Vo Nguyen Giap, *Tu Nhan Dan Ma Ra* (Coming from the People) (Hanoi, 1962), 168; Douglas Pike, *PAVN: People's Army of Vietnam* (Novato, Calif.: Presidio Press, 1986), 2.

51. Marr, *Vietnamese Tradition on Trial,* 247, citing Ha Thi Que, *Rung Yen The* (Hanoi, 1962) and Le Thi Nham Tuyet, *Phu Nu Viet Nam,* 214.

52. David G. Marr, *Vietnam 1945,* 213, 417.

53. Marr, *Vietnamese Tradition on Trial,* 247–48.

54. Duiker, *Sacred War,* 44–51; Herring, *America's Longest War,* 3–42.

55. Arlene Eisen, *Women and Revolution in Vietnam* (London: Zed Books, 1984), 29.

56. Duiker, *Sacred War,* 87.

57. Mai and Le, *Women in Viet Nam,* 163.

58. Ho Thi Bi, interview with author, Ho Chi Minh City, 14 November 1994, translated by Nguyen Thi Sau and Hung Tran. Bi's story, in the following paragraphs, is all from this interview. It was apparent that she had told her story many times, and she was considered a celebrity. An army photographer and a stenographer were on hand to record our interview.

59. Mai and Le, *Women in Viet Nam,* 161.

60. Jan Vansina, *Oral Tradition as History* (Madison: University of Wisconsin Press, 1985), 9.

61. Mai and Le, *Women in Viet Nam,* 161. One should note that although Mai and Le are invariably precise in their statistics, precision in statistics is an obsession among Party members and the authors cite different dates for some commonly known events. The evenness of the numbers and the absence of sources makes such statistics questionable.

62. Ibid., 158.

63. Visit to Con Dao (Poulo Condore) prison and museum, 18 February 1994. Nguyen Thi Sau translated for me.

64. Eisen, *Women and Revolution in Vietnam,* 29–30.

65. George McT. Kahin, *Intervention: How America Became Involved in Vietnam* (New York: Knopf, 1986), 62–64.

66. Luong Thi Trang, interview with author, Ben Tre, 9 November 1995, translated by Nguyen Thi Sau and Hung Tran.

67. Hoang Ngoc Nguyen, discussion with author, Salt Lake City, 22 August 1997.

68. Hy V. Luong, with Nguyen Dac Bang, *Revolution in the Village: Tradition and Transformation in North Vietnam, 1925–1988* (Honolulu: University of Hawaii Press, 1992), 156.

2. War in the Delta, War in the Jungles

1. Ronald H. Spector, *Advice and Support: The Early Years* (Washington, D.C.: Center for Military History, 1983).

2. William J. Duiker, *Sacred War: Nationalism and Revolution in a Divided Vietnam* (New York: McGraw-Hill, 1995), 120–23.

3. Mai Thi Tu and Le Thi Nham Tuyet, *Women in Viet Nam* (Hanoi: Foreign Languages, 1978), 81. The authors refer to Chinese support for one side during the Tay Son rebellion in the seventeenth century.

4. General overviews of the war can be found in Stanley Karnow, *Vietnam: A History* (1983; reprint, New York: Penguin, 1991); Philip Davidson, *Vietnam at War: The History, 1946–1975* (Novato, Calif.: Presidio Press, 1988); Gabriel Kolko, *Anatomy of a War: Vietnam, the United States, and the Modern Historical Experience* (New York: Pantheon, 1985); Marilyn B. Young, *The Vietnam Wars, 1945–1990* (New York: HarperCollins, 1991); and Duiker, *Sacred War*, to name but a few.

5. Douglas Pike, *Viet Cong: The Organization and Techniques of the National Liberation Front of South Vietnam* (Cambridge, Mass.: MIT Press, 1966), esp. 174–78. George McT. Kahin, *Intervention: How America Became Involved in Vietnam* (New York: Knopf, 1986), 114–17; Young, *Vietnam Wars*, 70–74.

6. For a diagram and explanations of the concept, see Douglas Pike, *PAVN: People's Army of Vietnam* (Novato, Calif.: Presidio Press, 1986), 112, chaps. 8–10. See also Pike, *Viet Cong*, and *War, Peace, and the Viet Cong* (Cambridge, Mass.: MIT Press, 1969).

7. Nancy Wiegertsma, *Vietnam: Peasant Land, Peasant Revolution: Patriarchy and Collectivity in the Rural Economy* (New York: St Martin's Press, 1988), 209.

8. Pike, *PAVN*, 212.

9. Ibid.; "The Viet Cong: The Front Techniques", April 1967, 21–22, Pike Collection, Texas Tech University, Lubbock. This document, probably prepared for American military use, states that the Lao Dong Party (Communist Party) dominated every level of an extensive pyramidal structure. The mass associations reported to the National Liberation Front of South Vietnam, but had parallel Party control channels to the hamlet self-defense militia and the village guerrillas and militia, two military units in which women fought. Obviously, these structures applied only where such an organization was "legal," or under the control of revolutionary forces—the NLF.

10. Le Thi Nham Tuyet, *The Vietnamese Women's Movement in Modern Times and the Significance of Women's Liberation in Vietnam* (Hanoi: Foreign Languages, 1978), 13.

11. Wiegertsma, *Vietnam,* 209.

12. "New Advances by the Southern Women's Movement," *Nhan Dan* (The People), 9 March 1970, 3, 4, Pike Collection.

13. Mai Thi Tu, *Nhong Tien Bo Moi Cua Phong Trao Phu Nu Mien Nam* (The Vietnamese Woman, Yesterday and Today), *Vietnamese Studies* (1966): 40.

14. Young, *Vietnam Wars,* 64, citing Phan Thi Nhu Banh, *Ta Thi Kieu, An Heroic Girl of Ben Tre* (Saigon: Liberation Editions, n.d.), 18.

15. Weigertsma, *Vietnam,* 210.

16. "Emulation in Developing a Strong and Stable Party in Order to Defeat U.S. Aggressors," Vietnam Captured Documents 1118, Pike Collection, 1967.

17. Ibid.

18. Ibid.

19. "Women's Liberation Association," 173–74, Pike Collection.

20. Ibid., 178. This document bears no author's name. However, Pike used this phrase in writings about the Viet Cong, and he may have written this piece.

21. This was its name during the French war. During the American war, the name was changed to Committee for the South, and it was led by Le Duan. The acronym COSVN was still in use, however. See Duiker, *Sacred War,* 101.

22. Nguyen Thi Dinh, "No Other Road to Take," recorded by Tran Huong Nam, translated by Mai Van Elliott, Data Paper 102, Southeast Asia Program, Cornell University, 1976.

23. Ibid., 1–2; William J. Duiker, in *The Communist Road to Power in Vietnam* (Boulder, Colo.: Westview Press, 1981), 18–19, does not relate this group specifically to Ben Tre; Ho himself was in Canton at that time.

24. Lady Borton, *After Sorrow: An American Among the Vietnamese* (New York: Viking, 1995), 75; "Women of the Liberation," editorial in *Phu Nu Giai Phong* (Liberation Women): The uprising took place on November 23, 1940. It was in this uprising that the heroine Nguyen Thi Minh Khai was captured by the French and subsequently executed. See Liberation Radio broadcast to South Vietnam, in Vietnamese, 23 November 1940, Pike Collection, Unit 5, 1971.

25. Information from Ben Tre Provincial Museum, Ben Tre, 10 November 1995.

26. Dinh, "No Other Road to Take," 28–36.

27. Ibid., 37–38.

28. This was the opinion of Dr. Duong Quynh Hoa, who knew Dinh well. Duong Quynh Hoa, interview with author, Ho Chi Minh City, 6 November 1995.

29. Dinh, "No Other Road to Take," 39–47.

30. Ibid., 59–65.

31. Borton relates the use of the wooden rifles to scare away the Diem soldiers in *After Sorrow,* 76–77.

32. The museum of the Vietnam Women's Union in Ho Chi Minh City has a large display of these wooden rifles. The story is recounted in Dinh "No Other Road to Take," and Kahin, *Intervention,* 112.

33. Young, *Vietnam Wars,* 66.

34. Ibid., 66–67; Dinh, "No Other Road to Take," 73–74.

35. William R. Andrews, *The Village War: Vietnamese Communist Revolutionary Activities in Dinh Tuong Province, 1960–1964* (Columbia: University of Missouri Press, 1973), 38. The Women's Liberation Association was formed in March 1961, according to Duiker, *Sacred War*, 144. He lists a number of activities that women were involved in from 1930 on, such as proselytizing, acting as clandestine informants, and serving as transportation workers. David G. Marr, *Vietnam 1945: the Quest for Power* (Berkeley: University of California Press, 1995), 416. Women's Union officials today state that their organization dates back to 1930, when the Indochinese Communist Party was formed.

36. Dinh, "No Other Road to Take," 77.

37. Neil Sheehan, *A Bright Shining Lie: John Paul Vann and America in Vietnam* (New York: Random House, 1988).

38. Quoted Christine Pelzer White, "Love, War, and Revolution: Reflections on the Memoirs of Nguyen Thi Dinh," *Indochina Newsletter*, March–April 1991, 8.

39. Borton, *After Sorrow*, 89.

40. Information from Ben Tre Provincial Museum, Ben Tre, Vietnam, 10 November 1995.

41. Nguyen Thi Thu, interview with author, Dinh Thuy, 6 November 1995, translated by Nguyen Thi Sau.

42. Borton, *After Sorrow*, 73.

43. Tu, "Vietnamese Women," 38.

44. Whether the term "long-haired warriors" was ever used for the women of the North is a matter of some contention. Although some historians assert that the appellation was also used for northern women, Douglas Pike and the women at the Museum of the Women's Union in Hanoi insist that it was used only in the South. Given the different roles that women in North and South played, plus the critical activities of Nguyen Thi Dinh and her followers, it is reasonable to assume that it was a southern term only. William Duiker disagrees.

3. From Uprising to Protracted War

1. People's Revolutionary Party, *Party Policy Toward Women* (n.p., 1961); Douglas Pike, *Viet Cong: The Organization and Techniques of the National Liberation Front of South Vietnam* (Cambridge, Mass.: MIT Press, 1966), 174.

2. Nguyen Khac Vien, ed., "Political Program of the South Viet Nam National Front for Liberation (1967)," *Vietnamese Studies* (1967) Pike Collection, Texas Tech University, Lubbock, 1967.

3. Luong Van Hy, with Nguyen Dac Bang, *Revolution in the Village: Tradition and Transformation in North Vietnam, 1925–1988* (Honolulu: University of Hawaii Press, 1992), 193.

4. David Hunt, "Organizing for Revolution in Vietnam: Study of a Mekong Delta Province," *Radical America* 8 (1984): 23.

5. Rand Corporation Interviews, File no. AG-134: woman proselyting cadre,

Phu Yen Province, December 1964, microfilm, Marriott Library, University of Utah, Salt Lake City.

6. Rand Corporation Interviews, File no. AG-243: woman liaison agent, Hue, July 1965.

7. Rand Corporation Interviews, File no. DT-164 (I): civilian rallier, Party member, and member of the Village Women's Association Executive Committee, Lo Ngang hamlet, Binh Duc village, 3 February 1967.

8. Rand Corporation Interviews, "Interviews Concerning the National Liberation Front of South Vietnam," File nos. AG-430, AG-II: unnamed informant, Sadec District, Vinh Long Province, May 1966.

9. Rand Corporation Interviews, "Interviews Concerning the National Liberation Front of South Vietnam," File no. AG-486: Ke Sach District, Ba Xuyen Province, September 1966.

10. Rand Corporation Interviews, "Interviews Concerning the National Liberation Front of South Vietnam," File no. AG-505: Vietnamese woman recruited in Cambodia, Tan Chau and An Phu Districts, An Giang Province, April 1967. The rest of her story appears in Chapter 4.

11. Hunt, "Organizing for Revolution in Vietnam," 143. Hunt used the DT series of the Rand interviews in his analysis of the revolutionary situation in the My Tho area. Ben Tre Province had been a hotbed of revolutionary activity since colonial times.

12. Pike, *Viet Cong*, 176.

13. John Penycate and Tom Mangold, *The Tunnels of Cu Chi* (1985; reprint, New York: Berkeley, 1986), 228–40.

14. Mary Ann Tétreault, "Vietnam," in *Women and Revolution in Africa, Asia, and the New World*, edited by Mary Ann Tétreault (Columbia: University of South Carolina Press, 1994), 121, citing Le Han Danh, "The Long-Haired Army," *Vietnamese Studies* 10 (1966): 61–62.

15. Mai Thi Tu and Le Thi Nham Tuyet, *Women of Viet Nam* (Hanoi: Foreign Languages, 1978), 148. The authors have two conflicting dates for the outbreak of the *dong khoi* in Ben Tre, including the participation of Nguyen Thi Dinh. The uprising was actually in 1960, not 1945; they use the correct date later in their writing.

16. Hunt, "Organizing for Revolution in Vietnam," 75.

17. "Supplementing the Directive No. 13 TC (possibly COSVN) on the Establishment of Government," no. 458/RY12, Pike Collection, 1968.

18. Ibid.

19. Rand Corporation Interviews, "Interviews Concerning the National Liberation Front of South Vietnam," File no. AG-505, April 1967.

20. Pike, *Viet Cong*, 178.

21. "Women's Association of Quang Ngai Province, VC Region 5," Pike Collection, NLF, 1970.

22. Rand Corporation Interviews, "Troop Training and Combat Competition Campaign—An Emulation Plan," reel 2, frame 0315, Document no. 15, January 1969.

23. "Complete Report: (Activities of the [Binh Dinh] Province Forward Supply Council in 1965," Document no. 08-1195-66, Pike Collection, NLF, 1966–1967.

24. Duiker, *Sacred War*, 145.

25. Ibid.

26. "Agencies of Binh Dinh Province Party Committee, Region 5," Document no. 03-2840-70, Pike Collection, 1970.

27. Militia Subsection, Staff Section, Ninh Thuan Province Unit, "Militia Activities During the First Six Months of 1966," 22 June 1966, Pike Collection, 1966.

28. "VC Unit 70 Bi-annual (1965–1966) Report on Achievements in Quang Nam Province," 8 May 1967, Document no. 05-2581-67, Pike Collection, 1966–1967; James Wirtz, *The Tet Offensive: Intelligence Failure in War* (Ithaca, N.Y.: Cornell University Press, 1991), 118, citing Commander, United States Military Assistance Command, Vietnam, *Command History, 1967*, 3 vols. (Saigon: USMACV, 1968).

29. South Vietnam Information Service, "South Viet Nam Women on the Front of the Anti-US Struggle," March 1970, Pike Collection, 1970.

30. Major Richard L. Williams, "Development of Political Struggle Elements, VC Binh-Dinh Province Party Committee, VC region 5. CD Log No. 03-1028-72," Pike Collection, 1971.

31. Saigon-Gia Dinh Regional Committee of the People's Revolutionary Party, appeal to members in the Cu Chi District, 15 June 1966, Document no. 01-1380-6, Pike Collection, 1966.

32. Rand Corporation Interviews, "Interviews Concerning the NLF," File no. AG-505, April 1967.

33. "Women's Association of Quang Ngai Province, VC Region 5: A Report Prepared by the Executive Committee of the Women's Association," Pike Collection, 1970.

34. Edwin E. Moise, *Tonkin Gulf and the Escalation of the Vietnam War* (Chapel Hill: University of North Carolina Press, 1995), 82–91, 106–42.

35. Duiker, *Sacred War*, 166–72.

36. Le Thi Nham Tuyet, "Vietnamese Women Soldiers During and After the War" (Manuscript), 1.

37. Ibid.

38. Rand Corporation Interviews, File no. DT-164, 3 February 1967.

39. "Vietcong Tells Girl Recruits to Make War, Not Love," *Washington Post*, 13 March 1969, Pike Collection, 1969.

40. James Walker Trullinger, Jr., *Village at War: An Account of Revolution in Vietnam* (New York: Longman, 1980), 103.

41. Hoang Ngoc Nguyen, discussion with author, Salt Lake City, 10 November 1997.

42. Interview with captured prisoner, NLF, 1973–1976, Pike Collection.

43. Rand Corporation Interview, File no. DT-164, 3 February 1967.

44. Rand Corporation Interviews, File no. AG-505, April 1967.

45. Ho Anh Tai, "Fragment of a Man," in *The Other Side of Heaven: Postwar Fiction by Vietnamese and American Writers*, edited by Wayne Karlin, Le Minh Khue, and Truong Vu (Willimantic, Conn.: Curbstone Press, 1995), 33–34.

46. Ibid., 33–51.

47. Rand Corporation Interviews, File no. AG-505, April 1967.

48. National Liberation Front, Document no. 933, Pike Collection, NLF, Unit 5, 1971.

49. Interview with Nguyen Dinh Chi, "Women's Struggle Movement Increasing in South," *Phu Nu Vietnam* (Women of Vietnam), 1 November 1969, 19–20, Pike Collection, NLF-ORG, Unit 5, 1969.

50. "Women Mobilizing Cadres Conference Issues Communiqué," Liberation Radio broadcast to South Vietnam, in Vietnamese, 18 February 1970, Pike Collection, NLF, Unit 5, 1970. This refrain was repeated on Liberation Radio in an address broadcast on 20 February.

51. Provisional Revolutionary Government, "Security Tasks in 1970" 8/b/NP, I: "Situation Analysis," Document no. 1043, Pike Collection, Unit 5, 1970.

52. "LPA Reports Recent Military Events in South Vietnam," Liberation Press Agency broadcast to Eastern Europe and the Far East, in English, 1 August 1972, Document no. 1113, Pike Collection, NLF, Unit 5, 1972; "Regimentation and Rape," *Red Regime Preview*, Document no. 001122, Pike Collection, NLF, Unit 5, 1972.

53. Susan Brownmiller, *Against Our Will: Men, Women, and Rape* (New York: Fawcett, 1993).

54. Interview with a defector, "The Disunion Between North and South Elements in the Communist 9th Work Site Division," April 1974, Pike Collection, Unit 5, 1973–1976.

55. "Report: Reform Camps 50-D and T-101 and Psywar Vulnerabilities," January 1974, Pike Collection, Unit 5, 1973–1976.

56. Truong Nhu Tang, with David Chanoff and Doan Van Toai, *A Vietcong Memoir* (San Diego, Calif.: Harcourt Brace Jovanovich, 1985), 66–69.

57. Ibid., 180–81; Duong Quynh Hoa, interview with author, Ho Chi Minh City, 7 November 1995.

58. Women's Union of Quang Nam, *Phong Trao Phu Nu: Quang Nam-Da Nang, 1954–1975* (History of the Women's Movement in Quang Nam-Da Nang, 1954–1975) (Da Nang: Women's Union, 1995), 77–78, translated by Thanh Quang Huynh.

59. Ibid., 79–85.

60. Ibid., 91–92.

61. Ibid., 141–42.

4. The Long-Haired Warriors

1. Mai Thi Tu and Le Thi Nham Tuyet, *Women of Viet Nam* (Hanoi: Foreign Languages, 1978), 179.

2. Ibid., 190–91.

3. "Valiant on the Frontline Dedicated in the Rear" [Viet Cong magazine in English], April 1967, 9, Pike Collection, Texas Tech University, Lubbock, NLF,

NLF-ORG, Unit 5, 1966–1967. Numbers vary dramatically, and other sources indicate the number was far fewer.

4. Members of the Women's Liberation Association in the southern Mekong Delta reported with amusement how Americans thought that all Communists dressed in black pajamas. So when they wished to go into a village and mingle with the crowd, they wore a white shirt, often the only one the village owned. Then they appeared to the Americans to be neutral or supporters of the Saigon regime.

5. Mai and Le, *Women of Viet Nam*, 191. Women shooting down planes most often occurred in the North, as American pilots flew low to bomb the cities.

6. Duong Quynh Hoa, interviews with author, Ho Chi Minh City, 28 February 1994, 7 November 1995. See also Truong Nhu Tang, with David Chanoff and Doan Van Toai, *A Vietcong Memoir* (San Diego, Calif.: Harcourt Brace Jovanovich, 1985), 132–33, 135, 149, 180–81, and William J. Duiker, *The Communist Road to Power in Vietnam* (Boulder, Colo.: Westview Press, 1981), 213.

7. Vo Thi Thang, interview with author, Hanoi, 6 November 1994.

8. Dan Thi So, interview with author, Dien Nam, 18 November 1995, translated by Nguyen Thi Sau.

9. "1968: A Year of Urban People's Crushing Uprisings and Continuous Attacks," *South Viet Nam in Struggle*, 15 January, 1969, 3. This story is repeated in many places, especially in captured documents from the North.

10. Pham Thi Tao, interview with author, Da Nang, 19 November 1995, translated by Nguyen Thi Sau.

11. For a cogent discussion of revenge as a motive for fighting, see Jonathan Shay, *Achilles in Vietnam: Combat Trauma and the Undoing of Character* (New York: Touchstone, 1994), esp. 133–35, chaps. 4–5.

12. See, for example, Rand Corporation Interviews, File no. 149: Tuy Hoa police station, April 1965.

13. Joint United States Public Affairs Office, Saigon. "The People's Revolutionary Party in Rural Areas," *Viet Nam Documents and Research Notes*, no. 6, October 1967, Pike Collection.

14. Mayor of Thuy Phuong, interview with author, Than Tien-Hue District, 24 November 1995, translated by Nguyen Thi Sau.

15. David Hunt, "Organizing for Revolution in Vietnam: Study of a Mekong Delta Province," *Radical America* 8 (1984): 147–48.

16. Nguyen Thi Bao and Nguyen Thi Hanh, interviews with author, Ho Chi Minh City, 12 February 1994, translated by Eli Cawley and various family members. These peasant women, who now live in the city, were liaison agents for the Front throughout the war. Hanh was present when Nguyen Van Troi attempted to assassinate Secretary of Defense Robert McNamara during a visit made to Saigon.

17. Le Han Danh, "The Long-Haired Army," *Vietnam Studies* 10 (1966): 61–62.

18. "Fierce Fight by the Long-haired Army," *South Viet Nam in Struggle* 25 (1969): 7.

19. Nguyen Thi Dinh, "No Other Road to Take," recorded by Tran Huong Nam, translated by Mai Van Elliott, Data Paper 102, Southeast Asia Program, Cornell University, 1976.

20. William J. Duiker, *Sacred War: Nationalism and Revolution in a Divided Vietnam* (New York: McGraw-Hill, 1995). The term was first applied to the Ben Tre women and then extended to all women fighting for the NLF, according to Mary Ann Tétreault, "Vietnam," in *Women and Revolution in Africa, Asia, and the New World*, edited by Mary Ann Tétreault (Columbia: University of South Carolina Press, 1994), 121. Douglas Pike, conversation with author, Lubbock, Texas, 18 April 1996; Dinh Thi Van, interview with author, Hanoi, 27–28 November 1995, translated by Dao Ngoc Ninh.

21. *Phu Nu* (Hanoi: Vietnam Women's Union, 1990).

22. "Propaganda and Training Section, Saigon Gia-Dinh Area," part 3: "Policy of the Front Toward Women," 30 March 1966, 2–3, Pike Collection, NLF, Unit 5, 1966.

23. James Walker Trullinger, Jr., *Village at War: An Account of Revolution in Vietnam* (New York: Longman, 1980), 102, 103. Trullinger found several stories that circulated in the village he studied, My Thuy Phuong, part of Thua Thien Province, about seven miles southwest of Hue. One was of an old woman who assisted guerrillas in ambushing American soldiers; another, of three women who distracted GVN soldiers so that guerrillas could kill them.

24. "(On the Occasion of Women's International Day) Women Combatants of South Viet Nam, Hanoi," March 7, 1970, Pike Collection, Document no. 004754, NLF-ORG, 1970. Kan Lich was among the official delegates to Ho Chi Minh's funeral. She was listed as "Heroine of the South Viet Nam PLAF" in *South Viet Nam in Struggle*, 15 September 1969, 7. In "Activities of Women's Union Members in the Army," *Women of Vietnam* 1, 1997, p. 16, she was depicted as a colonel in a photo by Tran Son.

25. See the picture of women soldiers in the Viet Minh in Duiker, *Sacred War*, 65.

26. Members of Vietnam Women's Union, interviews with author, Thuy Phuong, 25 November 1995, translated by Nguyen Thi Sau and reviewed by Hung Tran.

27. Bernard Fall, *Street Without Joy* (New York: Stackpole, 1994).

28. Ibid.

29. Nguyen Thi Luong, interview with author, Thuy Phuong, 25 November 1995, translated by Nguyen Thi Sau and Hung Tran.

30. Le Thi Vit, interview with author, Thuy Phuong, 19 November 1995, translated by Nguyen Thi Sau and Hung Tran.

31. For a good discussion of the cross-over point, see Marilyn B. Young, *The Vietnam Wars, 1945–1990* (New York: HarperCollins, 1991), 214.

32. William Colby, with James McCargar, *Lost Victory: A Firsthand Account of America's Sixteen-Year Involvement in Vietnam* (Chicago: Contemporary Books, 1989), 280.

33. The picture of this incident, by photographer Eddie Adams, was one of the psychological turning points of the war, in terms of its impact on the American public. See Stanley Karnow, *Vietnam: A History* (New York: Penguin, 1991).

34. Beverly Deepe, "Political Spearhead Role? Women Build Viet Cong," *Christian Science Monitor*, 4 May 1968.

35. Ibid.

36. "From a 'top secret' transcript of resolutions passed by a Phu Yen Province Guerrilla Warfare Convention held in March 1965; document captured in August 1966 by 101st Airborne Brigade," Pike Collection, Unit 5, 1965–1966.

37. "From a Resolution dated April 1966 entitled 'Development of the People's Guerrilla Warfare Movement,'" Document no. 09-1265-66, Pike Collection, NLF, Unit 5, 1966.

38. There is much evidence to show that American soldiers were disturbed, at least initially, by killing women and children. This was not war as they knew it, nor was it the way in which they had been trained. See, for example, Richard L. Stevens, *Mission on the Ho Chi Minh Trail: Nature, Myth, and War in Viet Nam* (Norman: University of Oklahoma Press, 1995), 170. Stevens discusses a mission on the Ho Chi Minh Trail when the enemy included several women cooks; he and his partner had an illuminating discussion about whether they should kill them, and finally decided that if they had to, they would, since the women could, of course, kill them.

39. Ibid.

40. The literature on Tet is voluminous, including Duiker, *Sacred War*, 212–14; Stanley Karnow, *Vietnam: A History* (1983; reprint, New York: Penguin, 1991), 528–81; Phillip B. Davidson, *Vietnam at War: The History, 1946–1975* (Novato, Calif.: Presidio Press, 1988), chap. 18; and Young, *Vietnam Wars*, 214–25. Every book on the war devotes considerable space to Tet, the turning point of the American war.

41. "Women Mobilizing Cadres Conference Issues Communiqué," Liberation Radio broadcast to South Vietnam, in Vietnamese, 18 February 1970, Pike Collection, NLF-ORG, Unit 5, 1970.

42. Hoang Thi Khanh, interview with author, Ho Chi Minh City, 5 November 1995, translated by Nguyen Thi Sao and Hung Tran; Hoang Thi Khanh, "Female Labour and the Objectives of the Economic Development in Ho Chi Minh City," in *Vietnam's Women in Transition*, edited by Kathleen Barry (New York: St. Martin's Press, 1996), 185–90.

43. One who learned of Thieu Thi Tam's plight was a Frenchman, Marcel, who corresponded with her family and pressured the South Vietnamese government to let her go. After she was finally released, he eventually met her and they were married. Marcel and Thieu Thi Tam, interviews with Mel Halbach, Ho Chi Minh City, February 1994.

44. Six women who had been prisoners at Con Dao, interviews with author, Con Son, 17 February 1994, translated by Nguyen Thi Sau and others. On Con Dao, see Gloria Emerson, *Winners and Losers: Battles, Retreats, Gains, Losses, and Ruins from the Vietnam War* (1972; reprint, New York: Penguin, 1986), 344–46, and Holmes Brown and Don Luce, *Hostages of War: Saigon's Political Prisoners* (Washington, D.C.: Indochina Mobile Education Project, 1973), 14–15.

45. "Workers in South Vietnam, the Vanguard of the People's Uprising," Pike Collection, NLF-ORG, Unit 5, 1970.

46. This incident was reported briefly in Nguyen Thi Rao, "Southern Women Grateful for North's War Help" [speech], *Nhan Dan*, 8 March 1969, 3–4, Pike Collection, NLF-DRV, Unit 5, 1969.

47. Interview with Nguyen Dinh Chi, "Women's Struggle Movement Increasing in South," *Phu Nu Vietnam* (Women of Vietnam), 1 November 1969, 19–29, Pike Collection, NLF-ORG, Unit 5, 1969.

48. "Women's Contribution to War," Liberation Press Agency broadcast to Eastern Europe and the Far East, in English, 8 March 1969, Pike Collection, NLF-ORG, Unit 5, 1969.

49. Interview with Nguyen Dinh Chi, "Women's Struggle Movement." The Cao Dai sect was popular in Tay Ninh Province. It is a syncretist religion that worships Buddha, Jesus, Victor Hugo, and other deities.

50. The best account of the tunnels is in John Penycate and Tom Mangold, *The Tunnels of Cu Chi* (1985; reprint, New York: Berkeley, 1986).

51. Ibid., 229–32.

52. Ibid., 232–33.

53. Ibid., 234–36.

54. Vo Thi Mo's story is told in ibid., 228–40.

55. Ibid., 227–40.

56. Ibid., 237–40.

57. "Women Mobilizing Cadres Conference Issues Communiqué."

58. "New Advance by the Southern Women's Movement," *Nhan Dan* (The People), 9 March 1970, 3–4; Pike Collection, NLF-ORG, Unit 5, 1970.

59. Mayor of Thuy Phuong, interview with author, Than Thien-Hue District, 25 November 1995, translated by Nguyen Thi Sau.

60. "Women's Union Marks International Day, 9th Anniversary: Women's Union Meeting," Liberation Radio broadcast to South Vietnam, in Vietnamese, 8 March 1970.

61. Cynthia Enloe, "Women After Wars: Puzzles and Warnings," in *Vietnam's Women in Transition*, edited by Kathleen Barry (St. Martin's Press, 1996), p. 302.

62. Ibid.

63. *Truyen Thong Cach Mang Cua Phu Nu Nam Bo Thanh Dong* (The Revolutionary Tradition of Southern Women) (Ho Chi Minh City: Historical Research Association, 1989), 325–36. Translated by Thanh Quang Huynh.

64. Brown and Luce, *Hostages of War*, 69.

65. Ibid., 382–83.

5. Youth at War

1. "A Father-Son-Daughter Helicopter Hunting Team," *South Viet Nam in Struggle*, 1 January 1969, 7.

2. Nguyen Thi Bao, interview with author, Ho Chi Minh City, 4 February 1994, translated by Eli Cawley.

3. "Phan Thi Quyen to American Youth and Students," *South Viet Nam in Struggle,* 15 October 1969, 6.

4. Ngo Vinh Long, "Ngo Dinh Nhu (Madame Nhu)," in *Encyclopedia of the Vietnam War,* edited by Stanley I. Kutler (New York: Simon and Schuster and Prentice-Hall International, 1996), 359.

5. Frances FitzGerald, *Fire in the Lake* (1972; reprint, New York: Vintage, 1973), 128–29.

6. "Kim Phuc Address at Vietnam Veteran's Memorial November 11, 1996," http://gos.spc.edu/p/phuc.htm. The photo won a Pulitzer prize for Nick Ut. In 1984, Phan Thi Kim Phuc was ordered to Ho Chi Minh City to be used in propaganda films, and in 1986 she went to Cuba. There she met Huy Toan, and they married. They were invited to spend their honeymoon in Russia, and obtained political asylum in Toronto on their way back to Cuba. Kim Phuc has two children. She traveled to Washington, D.C., for Veteran's Day in 1995 and laid a wreath at the Vietnam Veterans Memorial. She said she bore no malice toward the pilot who dropped the bomb, but would urge him and all others to work for peace. After the ceremony, John Plummer stepped forward and told her that he had ordered the attack; he cried, asking for forgiveness. She told him, "It's all right. I forgive, I forgive."

7. FitzGerald, *Fire in the Lake,* 247.

8. Ibid., 247–48.

9. "To: Executive Committees of the Group Chapters Subordinate to H-180," Document no. 11, December 1967, Khanh Son. 25 April 1967; Pike Collection, Texas Tech University, Lubbock, NLF-ORG/Gen, Unit 5, Section 3, 1967.

10. Mai Thi Tu and Le Thi Nham Tuyet, *Women in Viet Nam* (Hanoi: Foreign Languages, 1978), 311–12.

11. Phan Van Ton, "Ho Chi Minh Revolutionary People's Youth Group, Assault Army, Loyal and Outstanding Successor to the South Vietnam Revolution," *Thanh Nien* (Revolutionary Youth), October 1973, 18–23, Document no. 004264, Party Activities and Government, Pike Collection.

12. "People's Revolutionary Party and NLF Spokesmen Attend Youth Group Congress," Liberation Press Agency Broadcast to South Vietnam, in Vietnamese, 23 October 1970, Pike Collection. [Report by an LPA correspondent in Central Trung Bo on the Second Congress held by the Central Trung Bo People's Revolutionary Youth Group.]

13. Province Youth Group Committee, "Projected Work to Be Undertaken by the People's Revolutionary Youth Group of Kien Tuong Province During the Fourth Quarter of 1966," 15 September 1966, Document no. 12-1006-66, Pike Collection, Unit 5, Section 3, 1966.

14. Vo Thi Chi, interview [videotaped] with Mel Halbach, Ho Chi Minh City, 5 March 1994, translated by Thieu Thi Tan.

15. Members of Vietnam Women's Union, interview with author, Hue, 20 November 1995, translated by Nguyen Thi Sau.

16. Holmes Brown and Don Luce, *Hostages of War: Saigon's Political Prisoners* (n.p., 1973), 69–70.

17. "Formation of Viet Cong Espionage Organization 'Trung Duong Poetical and Literary Group' Among Elementary and High School Students in Saigon," 28 February 1974, Document no. 004271, Pike Collection, CED 2/74, NLF-ORG/Gen, 1973–75.

18. Members of Vietnam Women's Union, interview with author, Dinh Thuy, 8 November 1995, translated by Nguyen Thi Sau.

19. Ngo Thi Bich Loi, interview with author, Hue, 23 November 1995, translated by Nguyen Thi Sau.

20. Le Ly Hayslip, with Jay Wurts, *When Heaven and Earth Changed Places: A Vietnamese Woman's Journey from War to Peace* (New York: Plume, 1993); Yung Krall, *A Thousand Tears Falling* (Atlanta: Longstreet Press, 1995).

21. These and other observations about Nguyen Thi Sau's life came from many conversations over the space of three years, 1992 to 1995.

22. Nguyen Thi Tinh, interview and conversation with author, Hanoi, mid-January 1992. At that time, Tinh was employed by the Vietnam–America Friendship Association.

23. Nguyen Khac Vien, *Southern Vietnam (1975–1985)* (Hanoi: Foreign Languages, 1985), 79, 109. Husband of Tran Thi Ly, interview with author, Da Nang, 22 November 1995. There were no dates available to me in either source for her life and death, but the story would place her arrest in the late 1950s.

24. Husband of Tran Thi Ly, interview with author, Da Nang, 22 November 1995, translated by Nguyen Thi Sau.

25. "Youth Increase Role in Support of PLAF," Liberation Radio broadcast to South Vietnam, in Vietnamese, 10 April 1969, Pike Collection, NLF-ORG, Unit 5, 1969.

26. "Not Marx, but Huckleberry Finn . . . Children in the Viet Cong," Vietnam Feature News Service, 16 (KTCB-075), April 1970, Document no. 004766, Pike Collection, NLF-ORG, 1970.

27. Nguyen Thi Rao, "Southern Women Grateful for North's War Help," [speech], *Nhan Dan* (The People), 8 March 1969, 3–4, Pike Collection, NLF-DRV, 1969.

28. "People's Revolutionary Party and NLF Spokesmen Attend Youth Group Congress."

29. Vietnam Feature News Service, April 1970, Pike Collection.

30. Stephen T. Hosmer, "The Communist Terror in South Vietnam: Excerpts from Viet Cong Repression and Its Implications for the Future," report prepared by the Advanced Research Projects Agency of the Rand Corporation, Document no. 001037, Pike Collection, NLF, Unit 5, 1972.

31. Eric M. Bergerud, *The Dynamics of Defeat: The Vietnam War in Hau Nghia Province* (Boulder, Colo.: Westview Press, 1991), 54–61.

32. "To: Executive Committees of the Group Chapters Subordinate to H-180," December 1967, Document no. 11, Pike Collection, NLF-ORG/Gen, Unit 5, 1967.

33. "Not Marx, but Huckleberry Finn . . . Children in the Viet Cong."

34. "Activity Plan, Binh Dinh Province Party Committee, VC Region 5," 30 November 1970, Pike Collection, NLF-GEN, 1972.

35. "Attempt to Form Children into Groups for VC Activities by the Teenagers and Children Proselyting Section, Sub-Region 1, COSVN," 13 January 1970, Pike Collection NLF-ORG, Unit 5, 1970.

36. Huynh Quang Tranh and Nguyen Thi Phuong, conversation with author, Salt Lake City, 9 March 1998.

37. Bergerud, *Dynamics of Defeat,* 55.

38. "Women in the Winter–Spring Campaign," *Viet Nam Documents and Research Notes,* no. 24, April 1968, Pike Collection, NLF-ORG/Mem, Unit 5, 1968.

39. Ibid.

40. Mai and Le, *Women in Viet Nam,* pp. 212–13.

41. Lew Ross, conversations with author, Salt Lake City, 1992–1995. Ross, a veteran from Bountiful, Utah, shared with me a photograph of several mountain tribeswomen carrying severed heads of their enemy, the Communist Vietnamese.

6. War in the North

1. The picture is displayed at the Women's Museum in Hanoi. The pilot returned to Vietnam and was reunited with the woman who captured him, a very sentimental meeting. He was downed in the Christmas bombing of 1972/1973 and was imprisoned in the so-called Hanoi Hilton. Information from Women's Museum.

2. Stanley Karnow, *Vietnam: A History* (1983; reprint, New York: Penguin, 1991), 160–61.

3. Ibid., 158.

4. William J. Duiker, *Sacred War: Nationalism and Revolution in a Divided Vietnam* (New York: McGraw-Hill, 1995), 87.

5. Karnow, *Vietnam,* 157.

6. Duiker, *Sacred War.* 144.

7. Bui Tin, *Following Ho Chi Minh: Memoirs of a North Vietnamese Colonel,* translated by Judy Stowe and Do Van (Honolulu: University of Hawaii Press, 1995), 5, 11.

8. Hue-Tam Ho Tai, *Radicalism and the Origins of the Vietnamese Revolution* (Cambridge, Mass.: Harvard University Press, 1992), 252–54.

9. Ibid., 88–113.

10. Institute of Social Sciences, Ho Chi Minh City, May 1998.

11. Ibid.

12. Bui Tin, *Following Ho Chi Minh,* 28.

13. Duong Thu Huong, with Phan Huy Duong and Nina McPherson, *Paradise of the Blind* (New York: Penguin, 1992) traces this time through the eyes of a family of three northern women. Although Huong had been an officer in the PAVN, Hanoi punished her severely for this less-than positive view of the regime.

14. Nancy Weigertsma, *Vietnam: Peasant Land, Peasant Revolution: Patriarchy and Collectivity in the Rural Economy* (New York: St. Martin's Press, 1988), 172–73.

15. Exhibit at Women's Museum, Hanoi; Mai Thi Tu and Le Thi Nham Tuyet, *Women of Viet Nam* (Hanoi: Foreign Languages, 1978), 270.

16. Mai and Le, *Women of Viet Nam*, 325.

17. Rand Corporation Interviews, File no. KO-1: military prisoner, NVA main force, regroupee, Party member, interview K-33, reel 1, June 1966, Marriott Library, University of Utah, Salt Lake City.

18. Lady Borton, author of *After Sorrow* (New York: Penguin, 1995), conversation with author, Hanoi, 25 November 1995.

19. Mai and Le, *Women of Viet Nam*, 258.

20. Ibid., 258–61.

21. Le Thi Nham Tuyet, "Vietnamese Women Soldiers During and After the War" (Manuscript), 2–3.

22. Exhibit at Women's Museum, Hanoi; museum staff, conversation with author.

23. Rand Corporation Interviews, K-33, June 1966.

24. Mai and Le, *Women of Viet Nam*, 2–3.

25. Duong Thu Huong, *Novel Without a Name* (New York: Morrow, 1995).

26. Mai and Le, *Women of Viet Nam*, supplement, 2–3.

27. Ibid., supplement, 2–4; "Vietnamese Women Soldiers," 265.

28. Vuong Thi Hanh, Vietnam Women's Union, interview with author, Hanoi, 10 February 1994.

29. Members of Hanoi Women's Union, conversation with author, 11 February 1994.

30. Nguyen Thi Phuong, conversation with author, Salt Lake City, 9 May 1998.

31. Mai and Le, *Women of Viet Nam*, supplement, 5.

32. Hoang Thi Chi, interview with author, Hanoi, 20 November 1995.

33. Hoang Thi Chi, interview with author, Hanoi, 26 November 1995.

34. Richard L. Stevens, *The Trail: A History of the Ho Chi Minh Trail and the Role of Nature in the War in Viet Nam* (New York: Garland, 1993), 68.

35. Ibid., 68.

36. Bich Thuan, "Women Gunners in Quang Binh," in *The Mountain Trail* (Hanoi: Vietnam Women's Union, 1970), 25–40.

37. Huu Mai, "The Mountain Trail," in ibid., 117–36.

38. Duiker, *Sacred War*, 203.

39. Nguyen Van Huynh, Vietnam Peace Committee, conversation with author, Hanoi, 27 November 1995.

40. Pham Thi Vien, interview with author, Women's Union, Hanoi, 11 February 1994, translated by Huang Cong Thuy of the Viet-My Association. Pham sat and stroked my hand, and said that I was the first American woman she had met since she went with a peace delegation to Czechoslovakia in 1968.

41. Pham Kim Hy, "The Lullaby," translated by Thanh Quang Huynh.

42. Mary Anne Tétreault, "Vietnam," in *Women and Revolution in Africa, Asia,*

and the New World, edited by Mary Ann Tétreault (Columbia: University of South Carolina Press, 1994), 122–23.

43. *Phu Nu* [Pamphlet of the South Vietnamese Women's Museum], 103.

44. Henry Kissinger, *White House Years* (Boston: Little Brown, 1979), 1024–25.

45. Nguyen Thi Binh, Conversation with author, Salt Lake City, 24 June 1991.

7. After the Shooting Stopped

1. Stanley Karnow, *Vietnam: A History* (1983; reprint, New York: Penguin, 1991), 547.

2. Ibid., 46.

3. Le Thi, "Women, Marriage, Family, and Gender Equality," in *Vietnam's Women in Transition*, edited by Kathleen Barry (New York: St. Martin's Press, 1996), 71–73.

4. It is interesting to note that there are no museums for women's history in the United States.

5. Holmes Brown and Don Luce, *Hostages of War: "Saigon's Political Prisoners"* (Washington, D.C.: Indochina Mobile Education Project, 1973), 36–42, 75–79.

6. Gloria Emerson, *Winners and Losers: Battles, Retreats, Gains, Losses, and Ruins from the Vietnam War* (1976; reprint, New York: Penguin, 1985), 343–48. Luce was forced out of Vietnam by the Diem regime shortly after this incident, but the publicity in the United States caused the regime to move the women to prisons on the mainland, at least temporarily. His account of his experiences on Con Son, the name used by the regimes of South Vietnam for the island, is in Brown and Luce, *Hostages of War*.

7. I traveled to the island of Con Dao with Nguyen Thi Sau, Eli Cawley, and Mel Halbach. Halbach's work on the island is part of his documentary *The Long-Haired Warriors*. We were there February 18–22, 1994. Halbach stayed for several more weeks with Thieu Thi Tam, her son, and her French husband. Halbach's film is available from the filmmaker at The Business Media Center, University of Utah.

8. Truong Nhu Tang with David Chanoff and Doan Van Toai, *A Vietcong Memoir* (San Diego, Calif.: Harcourt Brace Jovanovich, 1985).

9. Bui Tin, *Following Ho Chi Minh: Memoirs of a North Vietnamese Colonel*, translated by Judy Stowe and Do Van (Honolulu: University of Hawaii Press, 1995).

10. Luong Thi Kim Vinh, interview with author, Open University, Ho Chi Minh City, January 1992.

11. "Activities in Preparation for the 8th National Women's Congress," *Women of Vietnam*, Special Issue (Hanoi, n.d.): 15.

12. Thu Hanh, "Women Work for a Cleaner Environment," *Women of Vietnam*, Special Issue (Hanoi, n.d.): 26.

13. Bui Thi Kim Quy, Nguyen Thi Minh Hang, Nguyen Thi Phuong, conversations with author, Ho Chi Minh City and Salt Lake City, November 1994, December 1995, March 1998.

14. Kathleen Barry, "Introduction," in *Vietnam's Women in Transition*, edited by Barry, 6–7.

15. Ibid., 9.

GLOSSARY

• • • • • • • • • • • • • •

Army of the Republic of Vietnam (ARVN)   The army of non-Communist South Vietnam.

Chieu hoi   The "open-arms" program carried out by United States troops and ARVN to woo back captive northern Communists and Viet Cong and purge them of the "enemy" ideology.

Civilian Irregular Defense Group (CIDG)   The people's defense units organized by the United States in minority tribal areas of South Vietnam.

Dau tranh   Struggle, the basic concept of a people's war, composed of three components: *dich van,* or political action among the enemy; *binh van,* or political action among ARVN soldiers; and *dan van,* or political action among the people.

Democratic Republic of Vietnam (DRV)   Also known as North Vietnam, the Communist regime established in Hanoi in 1945 by Ho Chi Minh and reestablished in 1954 after the signing of the Geneva Accords, which ended the French war and divided the country along the seventeenth parallel.

Doi moi   The policy, adopted in 1986, of conversion of the economy to market-rather than command-based.

Dong khoi   Uprising, especially those led by the Communists in Ben Tre Province in 1960.

Government of Vietnam (GVN)   The regime based in Saigon and recognized by the United States as the legitimate ruling body in South Vietnam.

Indochinese Communist Party (ICP) The political party founded in 1930 by Ho Chi Minh, then known as Nguyen Ai Quoc.

National Liberation Front (NLF) Formally known as the Front for the Liberation of Vietnam, the primarily Communist group that advocated revolution and fought the guerrilla war in South Vietnam.

People's Army of Vietnam (PAVN) The army of Communist North Vietnam, referred to by the United States as the North Vietnamese Army (NVA).

People's Liberation Armed Forces (PLAF) The army of Communist South Vietnamese who were organized and trained as conventional and guerrilla forces.

People's Revolutionary Party The Marxist-Leninist political party founded in 1962 by North Vietnam to make sure that the National Liberation Front, whose members included thousands who were not members of the Communist Party, did not stray too far from Hanoi's direction.

Popular Forces The paramilitary units of the villages under the control of the government of South Vietnam.

Provisional Revolutionary Government Founded by the National Liberation Front and the Vietnamese Alliance of National, Democratic, and Peace Forces, it was regarded by the United States as a Communist front organization for North Vietnam, which demanded its inclusion in peace talks.

Punji stakes Sharpened bamboo poles often dipped in animal feces that were placed in camouflaged pits to wound soldiers who were passing overhead.

Tet The major holiday of the Vietnamese year, celebrating the lunar new year and falling between the last week of January and February 10, which in 1968 was the occasion of a major offensive by North Vietnam and the National Liberation Front against the armies of South Vietnam and the United States.

Viet Cong The slightly derogatory slang term used by the government of South Vietnam and the Americans for the Communist forces.

Viet Nam The traditional spelling of the country's name, which was combined by the Americans into one word, Vietnam, by which name the Socialist Republic of Vietnam has been known since 1975.

Vietnam Women's Union The organization for women established in 1976 with the merging of the Women's Liberation Association, of the former South Vietnam, and the Women's Union, of the former North Vietnam.

Vietnamese Alliance of National, Democratic, and Peace Forces (VANDPF) The group founded in 1968 by urban-based intellectuals, many of whom were not Communists but nationalists. Became part of the PRG.

Women's Liberation Association The mass organization of Communist and nationalist women in South Vietnam that infiltrated some legal groups, such as the Vietnamese Women's Association, the Women's Right to Life Association, and the Women's Dignity Association.

Women's Union The organization of women in North Vietnam, established by the Communist Party in 1945.

BIBLIOGRAPHIC ESSAY

• • • • • • • • • • • • •

   This book is based on several types of source material. To begin with, I used whatever secondary sources on the Vietnam War mentioned women—and few did. Those that did tended to generalize, listing in a few paragraphs the work that women did: cooking, nursing, caring for children and the land, working in intelligence and liaison, and the like. Rarely was there any mention of the use of weapons, other than crudely constructed mines or grenades. Historians of the American war, primarily male, did not know about Vietnamese women and saw the war from a male viewpoint. There are exceptions: Lady Borton, a field worker and director of the American Friends' Service Committee in Vietnam, whose latest book, *After Sorrow: An American Among the Vietnamese* (New York: Viking Penguin, 1975), is based on her deep knowledge and empathy with Vietnamese women, gained from having lived and worked among them for twenty-five years. But she is interested in the people, not the war. Marilyn B. Young, in *The Vietnam Wars, 1945–1990* (New York: HarperCollins, 1991), has some insightful observations, but her focus is on the conflicts and diplomacy of the wars. *Radicalism and the Origins of the Vietnamese Revolution* (Cambridge, Mass.: Harvard University Press, 1992) by Hue-Tam Ho Tai is very important for its deep understanding of Vietnamese feminism, although it is not primarily about women. Mary Ann Tétreault, editor of *Women and Revolution in Africa, Asia, and the New World* (Columbia: University of South Carolina Press, 1994) and the author of an essay on Vietnam in that volume, not only makes significant observations from a feminist perspective but has worked with women in Vietnam who have sharpened her insights. David G. Marr, in *Vietnamese Tradition*

• •

on Trial, 1920–1945 (Berkeley: University of California Press, 1981), provides significant and very useful background for the years of the American war. His latest work, *Vietnam–1945: The Quest for Power* (Berkeley: University of California Press, 1995), delves more deeply into the role of women in this critical year in the revolution. Other scholars, such as Douglas Pike and William J. Duiker, have recognized the role of women in the conflict, although they have mentioned them only in passing. Duiker's *Sacred War: Nationalism and Revolution in a Divided Vietnam* (New York: McGraw-Hill, 1995) is a significant contribution to the literature, treating the war from the Vietnamese point of view, and the author spends far more time than other scholars on the actions of women revolutionaries. Pike's *Viet Cong: The Organization and Techniques of the National Liberation Front of South Vietnam* (Cambridge, Mass.: MIT Press, 1966), although dated, is still a landmark in understanding America's enemy, and his few paragraphs on women are a teaser for the vast material he collected for the Indochina Archives (first at the University of California, Berkeley, and now at Texas Tech, Lubbock).

I conducted field research in Vietnam on several occasions, and even on those trips when that was not my primary purpose, I gathered stories, taped oral interviews that were translated at the time by Nguyen Thi Sau and transcribed later, and took copious notes on what I saw and the people I encountered. Most of my interviews were checked again in Salt Lake City with a Vietnamese-American student who verified the accuracy of the transcription. Whenever I visited the chapters of the Vietnam Women's Union, which I did on almost every trip, the women were invariably warm and courteous and were anxious to provide me with information about the projects they were currently undertaking for women—whether it was providing education and health care for rural women and minorities, advocating family planning, or warning women about the dangers of AIDS. They also talked about the past and their experiences in the war, although they preferred to focus on the future.

The interviews that I conducted in 1994 and 1995 were never totally satisfactory from the scholar's point of view. There was never enough time to obtain details, to return on another day for more stories, and to ask more probing questions. The cultural barrier prohibited the kind of interaction that would have occurred between two Americans, and I could not cross it. Borton, who lived and worked in the country for almost twenty-five years and was fluent in Vietnamese, became friends with women in two villages, North and South. She came far closer to understanding Vietnamese women, but as she explained to me, even with her background, research for *After Sorrow* was impeded by the women's Confucian heritage—along with the Party ideology and the governmental bureaucracy. The women were modest, she said, and regarded telling a story "as if it had some worth of its own [as] the epitome of arrogance." The women with whom I spoke did tell of their lives, but they appeared to speak not for themselves individually, but for all women, and they tried to make me understand that anyone who loved her country would have done the same during the war. Some women were not accustomed to talking and answering questions, knowing that someone would tell their story, but others were: they had been designated as heroines. Narrating personal accounts of their bravery and suffering and that of women around them served to elicit my commiseration. Although I was encouraged to ask follow-up questions in interviews, that was rarely possible, given the limits of time and energy. The stories were general, lacking detail, perhaps a cultural norm of the Vietnamese.

Visits to local museums sometimes filled in the gaps. An exhibition on the *dong khoi* (uprising) in Ben Tre not only fills the local museum, but provides considerable artifacts and photographs for the Women's Museum in Ho Chi Minh City. The captions give details for the events depicted, and pictures sometimes round out the story, occasionally in more graphic ways than I had wanted.

David Chanoff described several problems he had encountered in collecting oral histories for his works. He related that in interviewing for *Vietnam: A Portrait of Its People at War* (1987; reprint, London: Tauris, 1996), he recognized that secrecy had become a survival tool for the Vietnamese: "Survival requires silence and never letting anyone know where your heart is. They are suspicious of everyone and bestow confidences grudgingly." The only way around secretiveness, he believed, was to establish trust, which he found to be difficult when he lacked time. I faced the same problem and compensated, in part, by using my friendship with Nguyen Thi Sau, herself an example of the secretiveness of the Vietnamese. Over five years, after many hours of conversation and travel, I put together her real biography. But her guard was up; she rarely let secrets drop and did so only when she was tired or I was persistent. As a Westerner, I could not understand this behavior. At first, I attributed it to ideology—her dogmatic belief in Communism and the fear ingrained for half a century that openness could lead to betrayal and death. The use of pseudonyms, cover stories, omissions, and silence saved lives. She believed this not only from her own life and that of her family members, but probably in part from her education in Moscow. Later, I came to understand and accept such reticence and know that it was not directed specifically at me.

Pike has attributed the secrecy of the Vietnamese to their "singular inability to trust" and to the Confucian ethos that postulates a society based on right relationships: trust is conditional, since a relationship may change. Pike, who worked in Vietnam from 1960 to 1975, had no doubt that Vietnamese women were able to fight. They might have been relegated to second-class status by Vietnamese men, little better than the water buffalo they tended, but Pike pointed out in a conversation with me that I should remember that "the female of the species is more deadly than the male," an observation he attributed to Rudyard Kipling. He was sardonic, as he often is, but he believed his words. Borton, who would never have referred to Vietnamese women as water buffalo, also ascribed much of their reticence to the Confucian belief in right relationships.

Chanoff described another characteristic of the Vietnamese—their tendency to give only the essence of an event and to omit all the details that to a Westerner make a story interesting. He attributed this to their lack of interest in "hard fact and concrete detail." And worst of all, to him, were women, who were unwilling to talk at all to a foreign man. This was a gender difference that I did not encounter. Women were most comfortable without a tape recorder running, although some, who could speak English and knew that the nearby authorities did not, were not so hesitant.

The interviews conducted by the Rand Corporation from 1967 to 1971 with prionsers of war and defectors made up for the lack of detail in oral histories, since the interrogators asked endless questions. The goal of the Rand project was to determine why people would join the Viet Cong in the first place. In an appendix to his article "Organizing for Revolution in Vietnam," *Radical America* 8 (1974), David Hunt pointed out that the study was scarcely dispassionate: the interviewers were paid by the Department of Defense, and any account of atrocities committed by Americans or South Vietnamese was edited out. Since the defectors had either defected or been captured, they tried to present the National Liberation Front in the worst possible light. The interviews remained censored. However, they do offer useful information.

The most important archive of primary-source materials on the women of the National Liberation Front is the vast collection of papers amassed by Douglas Pike. Formerly the head of the Indochina Archive at the University of California, Berkeley, he moved to Texas Tech in July 1997. His materials were gathered over his fifteen-year Foreign Service assignment in Vietnam. He is the most authoritative source on the Viet Cong. But the contents of the collection vary widely in utility. Some materials, captured documents or transcripts of broadcasts by Liberation Radio, which was based in Hanoi, give instructions, orders, and exhortations. Others, translations from the *People's Daily,* are full of jargon and propaganda, which to the Communists is no bad thing. Reprints of speeches by Madame Nguyen Thi Binh and Nguyen Thi Dinh are also highly emotional. The contents of these materials, intended for a foreign audience, would lead the reader to conclude that all women were heroines who never broke ranks and never confessed under grievous torment. Torture is described in gruesome detail, and American troops are considered as guilty of it as the South Vietnamese.

The weekly newspaper *South Viet Nam in Struggle* contains more propagandistic information. It is full of emulation tales and news items stressing the solidarity of the Provisional Revolutionary Government with socialist bloc nations like Cuba. Events that disturbed the world, like the revelations of the Son My (My Lai) massacre, were covered in detail. The death of Ho Chi Minh also brought an outpouring of grief at home and abroad. But the utility of such pieces often lies in the collection of names—lesser-known women whose feats had garnered them a chestful of medals became official delegates to the funeral of Uncle Ho.

Much of the American material on the war at archives such as the Center for Military History in Washington, D.C., deals with military operations, which were outside the scope of this work. The "Vietnam Conflict" is perceived as an American war, with the Vietnamese simply stagehands. As Pike said, one must remember that 99 percent of the casualties were Vietnamese. The vast Echols Collection at Cornell

University appeared to have only one document on the Vietnam Women's Union, and it also was in the Pike Collection. No doubt, as the Vietnamese are collecting their own histories and building local museums throughout the land, more material will come to light. The archives in Hanoi are rich with material, and Vietnamese historians at the Historical Institute in that city are already working on it. Clearly, my work is but the tip of an iceberg.

INDEX

• • • • • • • • • • • • • • • •